About t

Dave Roberts has had over eighty jobs, including security guard, civil servant and KFC chef, in which role he was fired for trying to steal a sample of the secret recipe. After that, he settled for a career in advertising, which was eventually cut short by illness – but not before he had accidentally won a Silver Lion at Cannes.

Dave's first book, *e-luv: an internet romance*, came out in 2006 and was followed by *The Bromley Boys* (which was recently made into a film) two years later. In 2011, his third book, *32 Programmes*, was published and shortlisted for the William Hill Sports Book of the Year award. *Sad Men*, the tale of Dave's disastrous attempts to climb the advertising ladder, came out in 2014.

Dave's fifth book, *Home and Away*, was published in 2016 and tells the story of coming back to the UK after thirty-five years to find that everything had changed.

If you'd like to get in touch with the author, email him at wembley@daverobertsbooks.com, follow him on Twitter (@thebromleyboys) or visit his website (www.daverobertsbooks.com).

Praise for
The Long, Long Road to Wembley

'A story of love, dedication and hope. Roberts takes us to the very heart of his obsession with Bromley to show us that football has not lost its soul after all; it has merely been hiding. Beautifully written and underpinned by romance, generosity and humour, this is a book to lift the spirits. This is our national sport stripped bare and it still looks terrific.'

– Ian Ladyman, *Daily Mail*

'A colourful labour of love as one fan realises a lifelong dream of seeing his team at Wembley. Full of anecdotes, memories and stories that every football fan will be able to enjoy and relate to.'

– John Cross, *Daily Mirror*

'These are more than mere adventures in non-league football, charting Bromley's descent and rise again from a thrashing at Sutton, regular bashings by Barking, to the cup run which led back to Wembley after a 69-year absence. Rather, it marks the ups and downs of one man's relationship with his club, a tale tinged with despair and hope, love and excitement, humiliation and joy, with all the eccentric characters and colour of the amateur game, and a dodgy three-wheeled motor, thrown in for good measure. An absolute delight.'

– Dominic Fifield, *Guardian*

'A forensically recalled, life-affirming and affectionate tale of countless train stations, dubious musical tastes and – above all – never, ever losing faith in your football team.'

– Adam Hurrey, *Daily Telegraph*

'Football fan memoir is a crowded area, with often some scrappy and undistinguished stuff going on in midfield. But Roberts' tale of fraught but intense love has a charm and wit that sets it apart, with an eye for life beyond the touchline.'

– Stuart Maconie

'This beautifully written book is not just immersive but, in a football world that is now so money-driven, reminds us what the game is really all about: community, and common connections. Every fan will be able to relate.'

– Miguel Delaney, *Independent*

'Dave Roberts is the perfect lightning conductor for the vagaries of the football fan experience. Bromley are his team but such are the quality of his writing and the sharpness of his insight they represent all our teams. With a wit drier than

a Saharan wind Dave has us all living his dreams, disappoint-
ments and dodgy ideas with him, from the glamour of a rainy
away day at Workington to chip-based superstitions via an
outbreak of nudity in Wantage. Dangled in front of us
throughout is the prospect that tantalises every fan of every
club at every level: Wembley. The stadium's presence at the
end of the rainbow helps to make this book a heart-rending,
life-affirming joy.'

– Charlie Connelly, bestselling author of *Attention All Shipping*

'A delightful, half-century reminder of the toil, romance and
joy of football at another level.'

– Jack Rosser, *Evening Standard*

'Dave has captured a dream that came true – then turned into
a nightmare – but was ultimately a cherished dream that came
true – wonderful.'

– Ian 'Moose' Abrahams, talkSPORT

'Dave's epic journey with Bromley shows you real footballing
love. It's not all flowers but it's a deep, true emotional bond and
reminds us all that passion is not just about the Premier League.
I really enjoyed it.'

– Martin Lipton, *The Sun*

The Long, Long Road to Wembley

One man's fifty-year journey towards his ultimate football dream

Dave Roberts

unbound

This edition first published in 2019

Unbound
6th Floor Mutual House, 70 Conduit Street, London W1S 2GF
www.unbound.com
All rights reserved

ISBN (eBook): 978-1-78965-056-3
ISBN (Paperback): 978-1-78965-055-6

Cover design by Mecob

Printed and bound in Great Britain by Clays Ltd, Elcograf S.p.A.

This book is dedicated to my friend Roy Oliver –
a Bromley man through and through.

'Adventure. Excitement. A Bromley FC fan craves not these things.'

– *Garvo*

Unbound is the world's first crowdfunding publisher, established in 2011.

We believe that wonderful things can happen when you clear a path for people who share a passion. That's why we've built a platform that brings together readers and authors to crowdfund books they believe in – and give fresh ideas that don't fit the traditional mould the chance they deserve.

This book is in your hands because readers made it possible. Everyone who pledged their support is listed at the front of the book below. Join them by visiting unbound.com and supporting a book today.

Nick Evans
B R Stacey Fencing
Ben Fishwick
Stephen Fitz-Costa
Robert Fox
Peter Fraser
Roger French
Ray French
Stuart Fuller
Chamber Furniture
Lisa Ganley-Leal
Gareth The Bromley Club Cat
David Garwood
Roger Gascoigne
Stuart Glover
Bill Greenwood
David Gregory
Geoff Groves
Roy Haddon
Matt Hall
Duncan Hamilton
Kristoffer Harboe
Ian Harrington
Joshua Harrington
Chris Harvey
Georgina Hawkes
David Hayes
Tony Hayes
Mike Head
Col, Em & Mikey Head
Tj Herbert
Machel Hewitt
Jack Holland
Dave Hook
Mark Hunt
Jeff Hutton
Christopher Idle
Andrew Irving
Howard Jenkins
Carl Jones
Ian Jones
Alex Jones
Peter Jupp
Ian Kerr
Dan Kieran
Peter Knott

Dan Lambert
Quality Drainage Company Ltd,
Sarah Lawrence
Shaun Loughran
Ewen MacIntosh
Graeme Martin
Paul McKay
SR & AW Mills
John Mitchinson
Steve Moore
Doug Mortimer
Phil Munroe
Robert Murphy
Carlo Navato
Scott Nicholson
Scott Pack
Doug Parry
Geoff Percy
Billy Peters
Kenny Pieper
Justin Pollard
George Porter
Non-League Ranking
Keith Reay
Charlotte Rendell
Paul Richer
Dave Roberts
Tony Roberts
Steve Roberts
Catherine Robertson
Ewen Rose
Greg Rowe
Peter Rusbridge
Dave Rutnam
Rob Savage
Marie-Madeleine Scott
Robert Skudder
Andrew Smith
Neil Smith
Andrew Snowley
Amund Søderholm
Alan Soper
Alan Stonebridge
Jan Stöver
Mark Sturges
Donna Sussenbach

Rob Swaine
Jamie Thomas
Mark Tregent
Gary Tritton
Tony Walford
Richard Walker
Maurice Walker
David Wallis
Andy Warren

Georgina Weaver
Steve West
Tim Wheeler
Steve Whitehouse
Scott Williams
Geoff Williams
David Wills
Pete Woolnough
Paul Young

Part One

PROLOGUE

December 1968

At thirteen, I was already set in my ways.

Every time I went to watch Bromley, the team I was rapidly falling in love with, I'd go through the same turnstile (apart from the time when it was closed because a sparrow's nest had been found in the machinery and babies had hatched), and buy two programmes from the same boy (even though I knew him from the Scouts and didn't like him) and one Golden Goal ticket from a wild-haired man with thick glasses.

I then went to my usual seat on the bench behind the goal, convinced that my seating arrangements somehow influenced the game's outcome. This belief stemmed from the fact that new signing Alan Stonebridge had scored in four games running earlier in the season when I'd been sitting in that exact spot. I never sat anywhere else, even though the view of the far goal was unclear and Stonebridge's golden run had come to an end.

As soon as the whistle went for half-time, I'd leave the bench and head for the tea hut under the stand. There was already a queue inside because some people were apparently happy to sacrifice the (potentially vital) last few minutes of the half.

Although many of these wore Bromley scarves, I did not consider them to be proper supporters.

I was always a bit nervous standing just outside the door of the tea hut (the concrete steps were directly below the tannoy speaker, which wobbled unsteadily on windy days), but I was perfectly happy being stuck in a slow-moving queue once I got inside. This was because it gave me time to gaze lovingly at the tea-hut wall without attracting undue attention. It was here that about a dozen framed black and white photos of Bromley's 1949 FA Amateur Cup win were neatly displayed in a row. It was a reminder of the time when a huge crowd at Wembley saw Bromley defeat Romford 1-0 and 20,000 people crammed into the High Street back in Bromley to mob the team bus as they welcomed home their heroes.

The first picture in the row showed the teams being led out against a backdrop of huge banks of people. Proudly leading Bromley was chairman Charlie King – one of the few links to the present day. I had often seen him pushing a Silver Cross pram from Bickley to Bromley market square – a distance of several miles – during the week. I was impressed with his devotion to his family, until I learned that the baby wasn't alone in the pram – it also contained a hollowed-out compartment where he stashed the match-day takings in a leather bag before taking them to be deposited at Martin's Bank.

Other pictures on the wall included one of the coin toss, where a stern-looking Eric Fright, the Bromley captain, shakes hands with his Romford counterpart. Another showed a George Brown shot being saved by the diving Romford keeper. And, of course, there was a photograph of Tommy Hopper's goal that won the Cup, frozen in time forever.

But my clear favourite, and the one I was most reluctant to drag myself away from, showed Fright being held aloft by his Bromley teammates, proudly clutching the Amateur Cup, while another player was just staring, with joyous disbelief, at his medal against a backdrop of tens of thousands of cheering fans. I felt overwhelmed by emotion whenever I looked at it.

Thanks to an overactive imagination, all of these pictures would burst into life as I stared at them. I could almost hear the sound of 95,000 voices and the thud of the ball as it left Hopper's boot, crashing into the far corner of the net. I could hear the deafening roar as Princess Alice (a princess I'd never heard of before, but who had instantly become one of my top three royals) handed the trophy to a now-beaming Eric Fright.

He was one of my heroes, even though I'd never seen him play. Brown, who scored a hundred goals in that Cup-winning season, was another. As was Hopper, a bricklayer by day. I knew every player's occupation. And I knew every player's name by heart. I'd even looked several of them up in the phone directory, although I lost my nerve before I'd finished dialling the first number. Eric Fright was the easiest to find – he had a sporting goods shop near Bromley South station, which I often popped into, without buying anything.

The achievements of the Amateur Cup-winning team had awoken something in me. A powerful need. After seeing those photos, I knew that what I wanted most out of life was to watch Bromley play at Wembley. Whenever I thought of Wembley, I thought of twin towers, sunny days and Geoff Hurst. I thought of flags, community singing and footballers in suits walking around the pitch. But most of all, I thought of Bromley in 1949.

But since those golden days the same heights had never quite been reached – to put it mildly. By the late 1960s, Bromley were playing in front of just a few hundred people and the most exciting thing to happen in the High Street during the current 1968/69 season was when a monkey, owned by an engineer for a dry-cleaning firm, escaped and was found swinging from post to post at the Crown Wallpaper shop.

It was a universe away from the time when people stood six-deep on the pavement to welcome home the winners of the FA Amateur Cup. I dreamed of the day when history would repeat itself and colour photos of Alan Stonebridge, Eric Nottage and Jeff Bridge would take the place of the fading black and white pictures on the tea-hut wall.

I would normally get so caught up in my fantasies that I would miss the queue moving forwards. When this was abruptly brought to my attention, I reluctantly dragged myself towards the counter. It wasn't just being taken away from the pictures that bothered me. I was also nervous of the wasps that often swarmed around the iced buns.

The tea hut was run by one half of Bromley FC's power couple, Mrs Self. She ran a tight ship, serving a variety of sandwiches and cakes at reasonable prices, and made a good cup of tea. She was also official timekeeper at the annual five-a-side tournament that took place at Hayes Lane. Mr Self was in charge of the supporters' club and arranged coaches for away games, as well as writing a column in the programme. I was in awe of them and proud to be on 'hello' terms with both.

As I found myself face to face with Mrs Self, I asked for my usual slice of Battenberg cake and cup of tea (with two sugars). The cake's pink and yellow squares were always uneven, which shouldn't have bothered me, but it did. As well as this careless attention to detail, it was also a bit dry, but that doesn't matter so much when it's accompanied by a cup of tea.

I always made a point of taking the plate, cup, spoon and saucer back after finishing. I found it really annoying when people left them on the benches outside, and by the time the season was a couple of months old I'd added a new ritual to the ever-growing list. After the game, I went around the ground with a metal Double Diamond tray, collecting all the crockery and spoons that so-called supporters hadn't bothered returning.

And when I got back to the hut, Mrs Self always rewarded me with a grateful smile. Plus, I had another chance to see the photos on the wall and to try and overhear the reporters, who were filing their match reports after patiently queuing for the only public phone in Hayes Lane.

I was secretly hoping that Mrs Self would send me into the dressing rooms to collect the trays of half- and full-time tea, which had been provided to players on both sides. The referee and linesmen were also brought tea and, unlike the players, were treated to a plate of biscuits. I understood this. It was important to keep the officials happy.

I was feeling increasingly confident that reaching Wembley wasn't an impossible dream. The FA Amateur Cup was usually won by a team from the Isthmian League. Last season it had been Leytonstone, before that Enfield, and before that Wealdstone.

Plus, I knew I had time on my side for my ambition to be realised. I was, after all, only thirteen and, according to a science documentary someone at school had told me about, people of our age would live to around 130. Technology was so advanced, I learned, that someone in South Africa had recently had a heart-transplant operation.

The realisation that I would have another 117 years to see Bromley at Wembley filled me with optimism. The chances were good. And this wasn't the only reason I was excited about the future.

As was the case with so many people around the world, the forthcoming Apollo 8 mission to orbit the moon had captured my imagination. And, in anticipation of further space exploration, I'd introduced a Martian Subbuteo team to my collection, by painting the players green – all eight of them. The rest had either been eaten by my golden retriever Silas, been broken by being trodden on, or had been accidentally thrown away.

I got around this discrepancy in numbers by creating a scenario in which FIFA chairman Sir Stanley Rous decreed that, because of their superior physical attributes and ability to never get out of breath at high altitude (the next World Cup was being played in the rarefied air of Mexico), Martians had to play with eight players.

It turned out to be a calamitous error of judgement, as the green men lost every game heavily, usually to England, with Bromley's Alan Stonebridge contributing fifteen to twenty goals every time. The World Cup was now the Intergalactic Cup, with the final played at Wembley, obviously. Most of my fantasies seemed to revolve around Wembley.

And as autumn turned to winter, something happened that I'd looked forward to all year – the draw for the first round proper of the 1968/69 FA Amateur Cup was made. It was the first step on the long, long road to Wembley.

I'd been to the stadium once before, in 1966, to watch England play Germany in a schoolboy international that had been incredibly exciting. Alan Stonebridge had been to the even more exciting and slightly more famous meeting between the sides that year. I knew this because he'd told me personally. After each game, I climbed over the fence onto the pitch and bombarded him with questions. One of those questions had been: 'What was the best game you've ever been to?'

Was this going to be the season Stonebridge made it back to Wembley, this time as a player? I'd already tentatively asked my parents if I'd be allowed to go and watch the final if Bromley were playing and they said, 'We'll see'. Which was what they always said when they knew that I'd asked a ridiculous question.

After the draw was made, I had to wait another three days to find out who we were playing. That was because I had to wait for the next edition of the Bromley & Kentish Times to be published, as the *Guardian* didn't seem to consider the FA Amateur Cup first round draw important enough to print.

When I eventually found out that we had drawn high-flying Sutton away, I was only mildly demoralised, telling myself that you have to beat sides like that to reach the final. We'd played there a few months ago and lost 2-1 to a flukey last-minute goal. Sutton were definitely beatable and the good news was that Mr Self, the other half of Bromley's power couple, announced that the supporters' club would be running a coach to their ground.

Bromley were on the verge of making history. I just didn't realise what kind of history they were about to make.

CHAPTER ONE

I was dressed more suitably for a month's expedition to the North Pole than for an afternoon in Sutton.

Over my string vest (a craze that had swept school due to its alleged properties of trapping body heat) I wore one of my dad's M&S V-neck jumpers, my Scout jumper and, finally, my cricket jumper. I just about managed to zip up my green anorak over them. I also had my tracksuit bottoms on underneath my trousers and was wearing three pairs of socks (including my lucky ones). For once, I didn't protest when my mum wrapped a scarf around my neck and made me wear gloves and my sister's powder-blue bobble hat.

The first round of the FA Amateur Cup was one of the most exciting Saturdays of the season, but the weather had been terrible all week. Icy pavements and cold, biting winds made going to school an even more miserable experience than it already was. The one bright spot of the week came when it was announced that the Sutton v Bromley game was going ahead.

Bromley wouldn't be at full strength. Alan Bonney had somehow sustained an eye injury during an operation on his nose, Eric Nottage's famous right knee was yet again causing him problems and Kevin Sheehan was cup-tied, having played for Croydon Amateurs in the qualifying round. I wasn't overly worried as I'd managed to convince myself that we had enough strength in depth to cover these losses, even though this was patently untrue – our reserve team were bottom of their league and had fielded ten men in their last game. And one of those was the manager.

After writing out the likely team to take on Sutton, I was reassured. I'd had to bring the useless Phil Amato, who had originally been named as substitute, into the starting eleven, plus a couple of reserves I'd never heard of, but otherwise it looked fine. The fact that Alan Stonebridge was injury-free was the most important factor. He'd already scored twelve goals that season, including a breathtakingly good hat-trick against Grays Athletic three weeks before.

Satisfied, I made myself a large pot of tea (using two extra Typhoo tea bags), added milk and sugar, stirred it and poured the mixture into the Thermos flask. It wasn't the method that my parents used, but I found it ensured just the right strength. I then took two plastic bags from the kitchen drawer. In one, I placed both my sandwiches (each consisted of two Weetabix with thickly spread butter and Marmite in between them) and the other I left empty. I would use it later to protect the match programme from the adverse conditions.

'Be Prepared' wasn't just the Scouts' motto. They were the words I lived by.

I had even prepared a comment to shout out and impress my fellow fans with when the time was right. I'd noticed over the months that whenever a Bromley fan shouted something, especially if it was about the referee, it was met with laughter. I craved this reaction and had come up with what I considered to be a very funny comment based on the fact that our star winger, Eddie Green, wore contact lenses. It had come to me as I was drifting off to sleep one night and I excitedly jumped out of bed and ran over to my desk to write it down. It was hard to get to sleep afterwards.

This was what I'd come up with. At a future Bromley game, when a poor decision had been made, I would loudly shout, 'Oi Eddie, how about lending the ref your contact lenses?' I'd toyed with adding, 'He needs them more than you do,' but wondered if that made any sense.

But all this was stored away for later. For now, my sole focus was on getting to the top of my road, where the coach would be picking me up, without slipping over on the ice – although I was fairly sure that, even if I did have a fall, I'd be well protected by my numerous layers of clothing. Taking small, careful steps, I made it to the meeting point and then, when it arrived ten minutes later, onto the coach.

After greeting Stan the driver with a cheery 'Good afternoon', I found a seat near the front. This was where I liked to sit, just behind the three Peters sisters, who, as always, took up the front row. They looked identical. They must have been in their late seventies and dressed for the game as though they were going to church, with pearl necklaces and matching hats. I was a little scared of them; they permanently wore the same disapproving expression, which is bad enough when one person is looking at you boarding a coach, let alone three.

The Peters sisters had supported Bromley for just about their entire lives and had been to Wembley to see Eric Fright's team win the FA Amateur Cup in 1949. They had also been there when Bromley won it in 1938, at The Den. And, most impressive of all, they were present when Bromley lifted the trophy for the first time, in 1911, in a match played at West Norwood's ground in Herne Hill. All three of these finals had ended in a 1-0 Bromley victory. I could only dream of such a momentous result.

The Peters sisters were Bromley royalty and, every time I

saw them, they looked the part. People who normally swore a lot didn't dare when they were in the presence of the Peters sisters. I didn't swear at all, so didn't have to worry about watching my language.

This was my sixth supporters' club coach trip and my first to an Amateur Cup game. A couple of people had waved as I looked around before taking my seat next to Del, a shortish man in his mid-twenties. I knew his name because I used to see him, wearing a grey leather jacket with silver studs on the back spelling out the name DEL, when he parked his motorbike outside the Bromley ground. Having recently read a book about the Hell's Angels in California, I was a bit nervous sitting next to him.

I took out my copy of the latest *Shoot!* magazine and tried to start a conversation with Del about the cover star, David Webb. It wasn't long before we both ran out of things to say about the Chelsea hard man. I'd also brought along *Rover and Wizard*, which I'd bought because the cover promised a frame-by-frame illustrated analysis of Francis Lee's dramatic title-winning goal for Manchester City against Newcastle which had seen them crowned league champions in 1968. Lee had made his England debut that Wednesday. At Wembley, of course. We talked about that instead.

Our discussion was interrupted twice, firstly by the wild-haired man with thick glasses who sold me Golden Goal tickets at home games. It seemed he also had a money-raising scheme for away games – Pick the Score tickets. Potential scorelines were each typed on a piece of paper, which was folded over and stapled. If yours contained the correct score you won the jackpot of ten shillings.

I handed over sixpence, shut my eyes and picked my piece of paper from a large brown envelope with the name and address crossed out. When I opened it, I saw that I'd chosen Bromley to win 7-0 (or higher). Was this a sign? The scoreline was unlikely, but not as implausible as it seemed. Last week, Bromley had beaten Finchley 5-0, with four goals coming in a magical eleven-minute spell. Alan Stonebridge had scored one goal, made two others and hit the post.

The second interruption was by Mr Self, who was handing out coach tickets. After I paid him, he carefully filled out the words 'Mr D Roberts' on my ticket with his supporters' club pen and handed it to me. I put it in the plastic bag. Eager to build our friendship, I asked him how he thought we'd do. 'We could well surprise them,' he replied, with a knowing smile. I was encouraged until I remembered his programme notes before the Hillingdon Borough FA Cup game earlier in the season, when he'd said: 'We could well surprise these Southern League professionals.' We lost 7-0.

I would be happy with a draw today, especially as I overheard some alarming team news. Roy Philps, who was one of my favourite players up until that moment, had hurt his ankle in a Sunday League game which he was playing in despite being told to attend a special Amateur Cup training session. I hoped I never had to see him in a Bromley shirt again.

Another good reason for wanting a draw was that Apollo 8 was going to be launched next Saturday and, if the game needed a replay, I'd be able to watch the spacecraft launch on TV, followed by Bromley v Sutton. I couldn't imagine a better day than that.

When we arrived at frost-bound Gander Green Lane, forty minutes after leaving Bromley, it hadn't got any warmer. I looked around and saw naked trees standing alongside modest floodlights against a darkening sky. The pitch looked rock-hard. This was playing into Bromley's hands. Conditions can often be a great leveller. Plus, floodlights were always a source of pride for me. I often fantasised about Bamber Gascoigne on

University Challenge asking which was the first amateur club in the UK to have floodlights. 'Bromley,' I would reply, and he would say 'Correct' and award me ten points, while the audience gasped in astonishment at this unexpected answer.

I was pretty sure it was correct. The wild-haired Golden Goal man had told me and there was no reason to doubt him.

I bought two programmes, sealing one inside the plastic bag with the coach ticket. The Sutton programme was unique: it was printed on amber-coloured paper, a shade which reminded me of the custard we got with just about every pudding at school.

I had a special sub-section of my programme collection devoted solely to ones printed in team colours. Most people thought that Sutton, Wycombe and Corinthian Casuals were the only Isthmian League clubs to produce programmes like this. But they were wrong. There was another, less obvious, member of this exclusive club. In fact, if Bamber Gascoigne asked who it was, I could again shout 'Bromley' at the TV, and again be awarded ten points. Even though Bromley's programme, in common with the majority of clubs, was printed on white paper, blue print was used on the cover.

As I skipped through Sutton's programme, it wasn't long before I found the words of praise for my team that I was looking for. After mentioning the 1949 Cup-winning team, it went on to call Bromley 'one of the best amateur sides in the history of the game.' I could feel my chest puffing up with pride underneath several layers of jumpers.

Despite shivering, I had a warm feeling towards Sutton United. A feeling that lasted approximately four minutes.

I normally allocated the first few minutes of a game to assessing opposition weaknesses and working out where our manager, Micky Acland, had gone wrong in terms of team selection and tactics. But in this game, it was all over by then.

Within four minutes, Peter Drabwell (who'd scored a hat-trick in his last game) and Mick Mellows had put the home side 2-0 up, and Trevor Bladon had missed a sitter for Bromley.

By half-time, the lead had doubled, with Larry Pritchard and then Terry Howard helping themselves to goals (the latter's, in the forty-fifth minute, was actually quite a decent header) to make it 4-0. As I simultaneously sulked and marvelled at the Thermos flask's ability to keep tea piping hot without losing its flavour, I had to admit to myself that this season probably wouldn't see a triumphant return to Wembley for Bromley. There comes a time in every game like this where ambitions switch from glorious victory to damage limitation. In this case, keeping Sutton to single figures.

I was already preparing excuses for losing. It's always helpful to have someone to blame, and I felt that this was largely Roy Philps' fault. If he hadn't recklessly played in that stupid Sunday League game, things might well have been different. And another thing, the conditions, far from being a great leveller, clearly suited Sutton – although I had yet to establish how or why. My final excuse was that Bromley's players might well have been using the wrong studs for the hard, frozen surface. How else could you rationally explain why a team containing Alan Stonebridge hadn't yet had a shot on target?

I had barely had time to finish my tea when Sutton struck again. Their right back, fed up with having nothing to do defensively, pushed forward and beat Peter Higgins in the Bromley goal from close range. A few minutes later, it was six when Mellows added his second, with the Bromley defenders appealing in vain for offside. In my opinion, the referee, Mr R. F. Wood, was correct in allowing the goal, which prevented me from shouting out my contact lenses joke. Well, that and the gnawing suspicion that it wasn't quite as funny a line as I'd thought it was.

The seventh goal did not come as a surprise. Mellows set up Pritchard for an easy finish and Bladon made it 8-0 with fifteen minutes left.

I looked around me, amazed at the Bromley fans' capacity to remain expressionless as our team were humiliated. Maybe it was because I was younger than everyone else, but I couldn't hide my distress. I found myself slumped forward against the railing, bottom lip trembling, almost in tears.

There was no respite. It became 9-0 when Howard scored from a yard out and barely bothered celebrating. Only some heroic defending from Bromley prevented the score from reaching double figures.

History had been made all right. It was Bromley's record Amateur Cup defeat.

The coach was quiet on the way back, the Peters sisters, as always, keeping their thoughts to themselves. I did wonder, however, how they would report what had just unfolded to the fourth Peters sister, whose poor health apparently prevented her following the team that she loved.

Most people onboard seemed content to quietly reflect on what they had just witnessed. I had my copy of *Rover and Wizard* open, but it wasn't very good and I wouldn't be buying it again, even though the Francis Lee drawings were very accurate. I took out the match programme and noticed that it had the address and phone number of Sutton's manager, Mr Sydney Cann, on the front. I briefly considered ringing him when I got home to wish him luck for the next round, just to show that Bromley fans were sporting, but I wasn't feeling particularly sporting. I still felt in a state of shock and wished we had a manager like Mr Cann. He had not only taken Sutton to Wembley a few years earlier, but had also played in an FA Cup final for Manchester City.

I looked at my Pick the Score ticket and carefully folded it and put it in my plastic bag. It was possibly a collector's item, as this may have been the first time anyone had missed picking the correct score by a full sixteen goals.

After contributing my usual threepence to the collection for the driver, I got off the coach and arrived home just in time to see the end of *Doctor Who*, which seemed to be about Cybermen hiding in London's sewers. I couldn't really concentrate, as my mind was wandering, but I think they were using the sewers as a base for their invasion of Earth. It was while I was watching the end credits that I came to the conclusion that the most realistic chance of seeing Bromley play at Wembley was to climb into the TARDIS and make the journey back to 1949.

Things didn't get any better in the following days. News came out that Nick Howe was leaving Bromley to concentrate on his taxi business in Eastbourne and, delivering a fatal blow to my contact lens joke, Eddie Green announced his retirement. Rather than waste the joke, I tried it out on my sister, but she didn't get it.

Following the flurry of departures, Bromley reacted in a way that only Bromley could. The *Bromley & Kentish Times* announced one new signing, George Wilkerson, but he wasn't a player. He would be joining one of the countless committees at Bromley FC, following a stint as secretary of Beckenham Town.

It was a disaster. And, on top of everything else, losing so heavily meant that Bromley would have to play in the qualifying round next season – for the first time in over twenty years.

And then things took a turn for the worse.

CHAPTER TWO

The 9-0 humiliation at Sutton wasn't quite the one-off freak result I believed it to be at the time. In fact, it turned out to be an indicator of things to come. The following season, 1969/70, was comfortably the worst in the club's history, one in which dreams of Wembley were replaced by dreams of survival. In cold, hard statistics, Bromley won just three of their thirty-eight Isthmian League games, conceding 111 goals in the process. I only missed four of those games, and that was because I was stuck at boarding school in Sevenoaks.

It was now January 1971 and I had moved to my local grammar school. This meant, among other obvious benefits such as living at home again and having unfettered access to Weetabix-and-Marmite sandwiches, that I no longer missed any Bromley games. On top of this, I was pleased that I was seeing definite signs of progress. Small signs, admittedly.

For instance, during the previous season, we'd lost 8-0 at Barking. The same fixture this season had only resulted in a 7-0 defeat. During the previous season we finished bottom, just below Corinthian Casuals. This season we were second from bottom, just above Corinthian Casuals. A pattern was emerging of small, barely detectable improvements. The future looked bright, if a little distant.

All but a handful of players had abandoned the club, with a couple of decent players, for reasons best known to them-selves, having joined. And even more bafflingly, Roy Pettet, one of the best players in the Isthmian League, was one of four to stay. Graham Gaston and the Miles brothers, John and Mick, were the others. Because in Bromley's world, when you've conceded a record number of goals, the first thing a manager does is retain all but one of the defence for the following season (Micky Acland had departed by now and Alan Basham was the hapless man in the Bromley hot seat).

Off the field, things had been going a lot better.

At nearly sixteen, I felt I had developed a better sense of style than previously. Gone was the embarrassing multi-jumper-and-anorak combination for watching football on freezing cold days. In its place was a recently acquired sheepskin jacket. Or to be more accurate, a brand-new C&A fake-sheepskin car coat which, in my mind, was indistinguishable from the real sheepskin jackets worn across the football spectrum from fans to managers and commentators to hooligans.

I also felt much more a part of the club I loved. I'd spent much of the previous season working in the tea hut in the far corner of the ground and, towards the end of the campaign, had been rewarded by being allowed to work in the supporters' club hut. It was there that I was given the job I was born to do – sorting out the old programmes that were sold in the hut, from First Division games to Athenian League games, and arranging the display in alphabetical order. It was second nature to me.

And, crucially, I had now reached the age where I didn't have to beg my parents to be allowed to go to away games, although I frequently had to beg them to lend me the money to go to away games. As a result, I'd got to know some of the regulars on the coach.

Del, the leather-clad biker, turned out to be Derek, a married tax accountant, who now drove an Austin Princess and had recently moved into a maisonette just around the corner from me. I'd spent a season playing for his Sunday League team, Hayesford Park Reserves. This was a team so awful that it had to change its name and rejoin the league the following season under a new identity, Park United. I was not invited back.

Also in that team, and at every home and away Bromley game, was the wild-haired man with thick glasses who sold the Golden Goal tickets. He was a dustman called Roy and one of the worst footballers I had ever seen. He called me 'young David', which meant I was now greeted at home games with 'Golden Goal ticket, young David?', a personalised sales pitch which added to the psychological pressure to buy one.

Another man involved with the supporters' club was the mysterious Peter, whom I believed to be a spy, based on something I'd overheard. Of fairly average height, weight and appearance, which were no doubt an asset in his chosen profession, Peter was someone who quietly got on with life.

The other person I talked to on coach journeys was Davey, a large man in his early twenties, who was friendly with a ready smile – until it came to referees. He really hated referees, convinced there was some kind of Isthmian League-wide conspiracy to keep Bromley near the bottom of the table. The other possible explanation for our league position – that we were useless – never occurred to him.

The four of them – Derek, Roy, Peter and Davey – made up the card school near the back of the coach, away from the disapproving eyes of the Peters sisters. There were only two of them now: the third wasn't in the best of health and had missed quite a few trips recently.

We were all looking forward to the FA Amateur Cup draw, since the competition provided a welcome respite from the endless doom and gloom of the league. But when word reached me that we'd be playing St Albans City at home, my heart sank. St Albans were everything Bromley were not. A high-flying, free-scoring, super-organised team that conceded very few goals, with a manager who knew what he was doing. They were also amongst the favourites to win the Amateur Cup.

The only real hope I had was that we would get a delay of execution due to the terrible weather, so at lunchtime on Friday I cycled down to Hayes Lane to carry out a pitch inspection. I'd arranged to meet my friend The Grubby there. The Grubby was a morose hippy who had been in the year above me at school. We immediately bonded since we were the only Bromley fans there. We also shared a love of tea and, as a result, spent many an afternoon and evening on damp, splintery benches, sipping tea and watching Bromley lose.

The roads had been cleared of ice, so I got to the ground in good time. The Grubby was waiting by the open 'Players and Officials' gate. We sneaked in and saw the pitch was covered in snow. Leaving a trail of footprints which, I briefly worried, would be able to identify us, we made our way to the goalmouth in front of the bench end. Getting down on our haunches, we dug the snow away to reveal soft ground underneath. There was no doubt. The game would be going ahead.

There were two things I knew about St Albans. One was that their captain was called 'Chopper' Neville, a tough midfielder who reminded me of Nobby Stiles, mainly because his front teeth were missing. The other thing I knew about them was that Jack Dickerson had once played for them. Jack Dickerson, of course, being the referee in the 1911 FA Amateur Cup final, won by Bromley.

When Saturday came, I walked quickly up the drive to the ground, pumped up with excitement and anticipation, shouting 'Come on Bromley!' to no one in particular.

After buying my Golden Goal ticket and programmes, I sat down with The Grubby. He had a cup of tea waiting for me on the bench beside him. Honorary secretary Charlie King's programme notes didn't help our fragile confidence when he labelled our opponents 'a renowned cup fighting team and one of our league's strongest sides.' It also didn't help that our captain would be missing. 'Eric Nottage, who has his knee in plaster following his torn ligament, is certainly unable to play,' wrote Mr King.

The honorary secretary had recently returned from a Caribbean cruise, where his musical tastes had undergone a startling transformation. Gone was the familiar prematch marching band music, and in its place were the lilting reggae sounds of the Merrymen, whose easy-listening versions of songs like 'Yesterday' and 'Island in the Sun' drifted out of the tannoy to entertain the rain-soaked crowd.

It was a big game and there was a big crowd. There must have been at least 700 people packed inside Hayes Lane, many of whom wore blue and gold St Albans scarves. And they were the ones happiest as the match got underway, as their team were virtually camped inside the Bromley half. Our defence, especially Graham Gaston and John Miles, were having a torrid time.

Roger Grant had a shot cleared off the line by Mick Miles, and then Vic Lindsay made an almost impossible save from John Oxley. It was, in my opinion, even better than the Gordon Banks save from Pelé in the previous summer's World Cup. But Lindsay was finally beaten when Collett chipped the ball over his head from close range.

'Here we go again,' muttered The Grubby, taking the last

24

sip from his cup. But we managed to hold out until half-time, despite being totally outclassed. And then, just after the game got underway again, a free kick from Bromley's chunky winger Danny Lakey brushed Burgess's arm and referee Mr K. W. Sutcliff pointed to the spot. Giving Bromley a penalty was equivalent to giving Bromley a goal. Lakey simply never missed and he dutifully sent the St Albans keeper Trevor Howard the wrong way to level the scores.

Oxley restored the visitors' lead again on the hour with a far-post header, which The Grubby and I felt John Miles should have prevented. Not long after, Alan Basham removed him and replaced him with Mick Lloyd, a player I knew little about. But despite being 2-1 down, Bromley were playing really well, and were unrecognisable from the team that had been so useless in the first half. I felt that Basham must have given one of the best half-time team talks of his life.

In the seventy-fifth minute, Lakey's through ball found Jim Brown, Brown flicked the ball on to top scorer Tony Coppin, who casually chipped the ball over Howard and into the corner of the net. It was the kind of goal I always dreamed of scoring and it had been scored by the man who had effortlessly taken over from Alan Stonebridge as my favourite player. Bromley had pulled back to 2-2 and were looking better than I had ever seen them.

But five minutes later came disaster. An Oxley cross/shot was going wide when Danny McAllister slid in and, in trying to divert it wide of the post, side-footed the ball past Vic Lindsay and into his own net. The pain was indescribable. McAllister lay on the ground, face down in the mud, both hands clutching the back of his head as Lindsay stared at him in wounded disbelief.

It felt as though I was stuck in an endless cycle of despair followed by brief glimpses of hope, which was an accurate reflection of my life. But just as The Grubby and I were coming to terms with a narrow but glorious defeat, there was a dramatic end to the game.

Time was almost up when Coppin got the ball on the touch-line, crossed superbly and there was Lloyd to tap the ball past Howard for his fourth (and most important) goal of the season to make it Bromley 3 St Albans 3. Seconds after the restart, the whistle went for full-time and the players shook hands.

The Grubby and I were a lot more excited than they were. We scaled the wooden fence and dashed onto the pitch before running around in circles, releasing all the frustration of the past eighteen months. It was easily the best result of the season in what was easily the best game. Suddenly, we feared no one and couldn't wait for the replay.

Even having to write 'OG' next to McAllister's name in the programme didn't ruin the feeling of sheer exhilaration at getting the most impressive result of the entire FA Amateur Cup first round. As I walked past the grandstand, on my way to the tea hut, I saw the Peters sisters carefully folding the tartan blanket which had covered their legs during the game. They were beaming.

Mr Self encouraged booking coach travel by Thursday to ensure a seat for the return fixture but, as always, I booked at the office straight after I'd collected the cups, saucers and plates, fearful of missing out on the biggest Bromley game in years. The Grubby refused to go to away games. I'd never asked him why and he'd never volunteered an explanation.

The week dragged on, especially at school, as Saturday was all I could think about, which wasn't that unusual. The *Bromley & Kentish Times* had shocking news that Thursday though. Our most reliable defender (not a great claim to fame, admittedly), Mick Miles, was unavailable for the replay as he was getting married. The paper announced it was a 'more important fixture'. Well, that was a matter of opinion.

Although I was only a few months away from being old enough for marriage, I hadn't yet managed to get a proper girl-friend. The previous season, I'd suffered my first non-football-related heartbreak when my best friend Dave's sister had told me (via him) that she wanted to be just friends.

But time had partially healed the pain and I'd fallen in love again. This time with The Grubby's sister. I'd only spoken to her once, a couple of weeks ago. I was round at The Grubby's house, playing football in the garden. I'd gone to the toilet and saw her on the landing. She was beautiful, with big brown eyes and really good teeth. She wore a kaftan.

'Do you like living in West Wickham?' I asked.

'I suppose,' she said. I couldn't think of anything else to say, apart from 'I'd better go', and ran down the stairs back to the kickabout. I was silently cursing myself for not having applied an extra spray of Brut that morning.

As I climbed onto the coach to St Albans, I wished she could be with me, sitting together. Instead, I took a seat next to Davey, who would forever be known for what had happened at an FA Cup game at Bishop's Stortford a few months earlier, a match Bromley had lost 2-1.

Davey was getting increasingly agitated at the quantity of decisions going against us and was screaming abuse at the referee. As the final whistle went – early – a livid Davey announced that he was going to sort him out.

Showing impressive athleticism for a man of his size, he vaulted over the fence and ran towards the referee as he approached the tunnel. Davey was only yards away when he saw that the ref had stopped to have a chat with one of the linesmen. It was at this point that Davey suddenly developed a limp which slowed him down dramatically. As the small group of officials showed no signs of leaving the pitch, Davey stopped and clutched his leg, screaming in pain (I was sure he was holding the wrong leg), clearly hoping that they'd all vanish down the tunnel so he could save face. Finally, the referee walked off and Davey, whose limp underwent a spontaneous recovery, was left to describe what he would have done to him if only he'd been able to reach him in time.

But today the talk was all about the forthcoming game. Could Bromley once again shock their more glamorous opponents? And if we could beat St Albans, who had scored twenty goals in their last four games, surely we could beat anyone and make it all the way to Wembley?

It was a long journey – only Oxford City's ground among our regular Isthmian League opponents was further away – but not long after I'd had my Weetabix-and-Marmite sandwiches and cleared the resulting crumbs from my lap and seat, we arrived. It was a blustery, wet, overcast day and the terrace was uncovered, technically at least. It did also contain, bursting from one of the concrete steps, a giant oak tree, which provided shelter from the rain. The crowd was huge – at least twice as many as there had been at Hayes Lane the previous Saturday.

The terraces were quite slippery, a result of some leftover ice, and covered with acorns, but I wasn't anywhere near as careful with my footing as I had been at the Sutton game two years previously, since I'd recently discovered something that few people were aware of. When quizzing Mr Self over what benefits I got for my supporters' club membership, he finished by saying that it included insurance for injury at any ground Bromley were playing at. So if I slipped and hurt myself, I'd not only get time off school, but also get paid for it. Not bad for a subscription of ten pence a year.

I bought a couple of programmes and once again enjoyed reading praise for Bromley's Amateur Cup achievements. 'A very good cup fighting record' and 'they have won today's competition on three occasions' were just two of the phrases that leaped out of the 'Club Notes' page, although I was less happy to read that 'for the last four seasons Bromley have not had such good fortune and have found it difficult to maintain a good league position.' I felt it was unnecessary to comment on league performances in a programme for a cup game.

The game started with both teams having good chances. Jim Brown was unlucky not to give Bromley an early lead when Trevor Howard produced a superb save, but it was St Albans who opened the scoring when a Bobby Childs corner was nodded home by Chopper Neville, who celebrated with his trademark toothless grin. It became 2-0 minutes later through a spectacular diving header from Childs. Just after the break, Collett tapped the ball through McAllister's legs and it was 3-0. The contest was all but over, and the game entered a particularly drab period.

One or two of Bromley's less well-behaved supporters got bored and started lobbing acorns at Howard in the St Albans' goal. Avoiding them was the busiest he'd been for most of the second half.

Several of the better-behaved Bromley supporters had switched their attention to a game of hockey on an adjoining field. At the other end, John Butterworth added a fourth and the Wembley dreams were over for another season. Bromley had been well beaten. At least we'd avoided having stones thrown at the coach, which is what had happened to Hendon after their FA Cup win at Clarence Park earlier in the season. One of the few plusses of supporting such a useless team was that no one really hated Bromley.

The atmosphere on the coach home was surprisingly relaxed. We'd taken the mighty St Albans to a replay and, for the first half hour at least, were just as good as they were. Looking around me, I realised how much I loved these trips and these people. But I was already working on a plan that would mean the end of travelling on the supporters' club coach forever. And win over The Grubby's sister in the process.

CHAPTER THREE

I was officially an adult. I'd left school, got a job and had decided to buy my first car. The third of these major life changes had two purposes – to help me get a girlfriend and to allow me to drive to away games. I wanted to give something back. Derek and Peter had given me lifts all over London, and beyond, in all sorts of weather, asking for nothing in return. Wouldn't it be nice to let them relax as someone else did the driving for a change?

The only problem – and admittedly it was a big one – was that my seventeenth birthday was nearly two months away and I couldn't drive until then. The solution leaped out at me as I was looking through the pages of *Exchange and Mart* – a three-wheeler! Since I was old enough to drive one legally, it meant that I could be driving to Bromley's game at Leyton in the qualifying round of the FA Amateur Cup, which was our next away fixture. Plus, it was within my budget of £50 (including road tax).

The car was a Bond 875. I went to the library to read up more about it and, although *Autocar* magazine said that it was unstable at high speed, the verdict was generally positive. I rang the number in the advert, made an offer of £45 and the man said he'd drop it round on Sunday.

I decided to prepare for life as a car owner by getting a *London A–Z* from WH Smith. I spent hours poring over the maps, plotting routes to various Isthmian League grounds and, of course, to Wembley. But the first route I planned was to the Hare and Hounds Ground in Lea Bridge Road, home of Leyton FC. If all went according to plan, this would be the first time I'd be driving to an away game.

I then got a little carried away thinking about teams we might draw as we progressed in the competition and became a little anxious about getting to northern grounds. The complicated-looking Spaghetti Junction had just opened around Birmingham and even experienced drivers were getting lost and going around in circles. I was actually quite relieved when my dad told me that three-wheelers weren't allowed on motorways.

But football was only one reason for getting the car. The other reason, of course, was girls. Just about all the boys I knew who had cars also had girlfriends, and I was sure the Bond would be a great asset, especially with The Grubby's sister, Penny. I would often phone The Grubby when I knew he was out, hoping that she would answer and not their scary skinhead brother. And when she did, we ended up chatting for ages. I also dropped round when I knew she'd be in. I felt that owning a car would be enough to convince her to go out with me.

When I took delivery of the three-wheeler, I was less certain about this. It was an unpleasant shade of sun-faded red and was made almost entirely from fibreglass. There weren't seats by the standard definition, but a small bench stretching across from metal door to metal door.

I rang Dave – another friend with a sister I was in love with – to see if he fancied going for a spin. He said that he did and a short while later was sitting alongside me in my first-ever car. I loved the feeling I got from slowly accelerating and I soon wanted more.

I put my foot down and shouted out 'Steve McQueen!' as we took a corner, this being a reference to *Le Mans*, a film we'd seen a few weeks beforehand. However, McQueen, or rather his character, Michael Delaney, had the benefit of four wheels and was driving a Porsche 917, which was designed for racing at high speed. I was driving a Bond 875, which had three wheels and had been designed for more sedate activities, like going to the bowls club on a Saturday morning.

As the speed increased, the car began to gently rock from side to side, a motion that gradually became more violent. I was amused by Dave's nervous discomfort as I knew something that he didn't – that I was fully in control. I first started to share his doubts when I found myself wrestling with the steering wheel as the Bond began to lurch wildly and then took off, spinning viciously in a series of somersaults. As we scraped along the road upside down and at high speed, the screeching sound of fibreglass against tarmac, mixed with breaking glass, was horrendous.

When we finally slowed to a halt, at least a hundred yards away from where we had first overturned, people rushed out from their houses to help. We both scrambled out through where the rear window should have been. Our rescuers turned the car the right way up, and that's when one of them noticed that the roof had sheared off completely. How it had stayed in place to protect us, we never knew.

There was one thing I had to do when I got home, apart from confess what had happened to my parents, and that was to ring Mr Self and tell him I would need to book a seat on the coach for the Leyton game. I was hoping that no one onboard would remember my comments about giving myself more independence and offering lifts to at least a dozen people.

Being a creature of habit, I still took a Thermos flask to away games, and still took a plastic bag for programmes, but one thing had changed – I no longer brought comics. I felt I was too old to read them, in public anyway. Instead, I took a copy of the *Guardian*, a newspaper I'd originally started buying on the way to The Grubby's one afternoon in an attempt to impress Penny with my interest in world affairs, before discovering I liked reading it.

As I leafed through its pages en route to Leyton, I was drawn to a story on Mariner 9, the spacecraft that was orbiting Mars looking for signs of life. Unfortunately, a cloud of red dust surrounding the planet meant that the cameras couldn't see anything. But although I couldn't rule out the existence of goalposts with absolute certainty, it felt less likely at sixteen than it had when I was thirteen.

I put the paper down when I heard Roy shout the familiar words: 'Young David, come here and lose some money!' I heard this from him on most coach trips – it meant that one of the regular card school had either lost interest, or too much money, and a substitute was needed.

Since I didn't really understand how to play gin rummy, I never did well either, and before long I had been cleaned out. Instead of going back to my seat, I went and sat next to Mrs Knott, something I'd been meaning to do for ages. Mrs Knott was a young man in his late teens who had been given the nickname by Derek, on account of his long hair. His real name was Peter Knott. Everyone apart from Derek called him Knotty.

Knotty didn't seem to belong on a coach of non-league football fans. He was handsome, worked in advertising at a trendy London agency (Hobson Bates and Partners) and was dressed stylishly in a three-quarter-length grey herringbone coat, which made me a little self-conscious about my fake sheepskin jacket. He had a neatly trimmed beard, a pea-green shirt with large, rounded collars and a hooped Fair Isle jumper. On coach journeys he tended to sit alone and stare moodily out of the window, much too cool for cards. I desperately wanted to be like him.

As we talked, he admitted to a strange habit of plotting how Bromley were going to win the Amateur Cup after the draw for the first round was published every season. He'd go through each tie and cross out teams that he felt would lose, before carrying out a draw of his own for the next round and so on and so on. This was thrilling for me to hear; I thought I was the only person in Bromley to indulge in these sorts of routines.

We were both fairly upbeat about our chances against Leyton, and that was hardly surprising. It was easily the strongest Bromley side either of us could remember. So good, in fact, that striker Jim Brown was wanted by two League clubs, Charlton and Luton, while Southern League Dartford had made an offer for top scorer Tony Coppin. Coppin, who had scored six times in the last three games, turned them down because he had to work as a printer on Saturday mornings (Dartford had lost their leading scorer, Tony Nicholas, because he didn't like having to train).

Leyton were in the Athenian League and the first thing I found out from the programme was that they had no supporters' club, despite being London's second-oldest team and having won the FA Amateur Cup twice. Reading through the notes of Mr Bays, Leyton's honorary secretary, I discovered that writing them had made him dredge up some unresolved issues about an event that had happened twenty years ago. 'We played Bromley in the Amateur Cup in 1952/53,' he wrote, 'and I was reminded that we lost to them and that Harry Dixon played after declaring himself fit to play and should not have played and so we were soon down to ten men.' Then came a magnificent twist in the tail. 'I remember this well because I was there to play instead of him should he have been unfit.'

Confusingly, Leyton, like Bromley, were known as the Lilywhites. Even more confusingly, they played in blue, while Bromley played in red. The game kicked off at 2.15 p.m., on account of the government's power cuts, which prevented the home side from using floodlights, and it soon became obvious that Bromley were in a different class. It was a welcome novelty to feel relaxed while watching my team. The Miles brothers looked to have things well under control at the back, Roy Pettet and Ray Hutchins also caught the eye and our in-demand strikers looked like scoring at will. So when Jim Brown (or 'Slim Jim' as I had nicknamed him) opened the scoring after twenty minutes, putting a free kick well beyond Grant in the Leyton goal, it came as little surprise. Then it was Coppin's turn to slot the ball past the keeper. After Leyton pulled back a flukey goal, Slim Jim dribbled his way through the defence to set up Coppin to make it 3-1. As the final whistle went, I climbed over the fence, headed straight for Jim Brown and shook his hand. 'Well played, Jim,' was all I needed to say.

As the *Bromley & Kentish Times* said in its match report, 'Brown played like six men – and probably Leyton's bewildered defence thought there were six of him!' No wonder Charlton and Luton wanted him.

On the way home, I found that Knotty and I had even more in common. Music. As I suspected (the hair was a giveaway), he was a fan of Van Morrison, Free and Joe Cocker. I was able to discuss their records in great detail. Not because I liked any of them, I didn't, but because The Grubby forced me to listen to them all when I was round at his house, ignoring my protests.

Knotty then dropped a major bombshell. He casually mentioned that he had famous cousins, with whom he hung out regularly. One, Alan, was rhythm guitarist for the Tremeloes ('Silence is Golden' was one of my favourite singles) and another, Mike, was drummer for Christie ('Yellow River' was also one of my favourite singles).

This was one of the most exciting things I had ever heard. I spent the rest of the journey home interrogating him, demanding an insider's tales of Christie and the Tremeloes, hinting heavily that I wouldn't mind coming along next time they went for a drink. In my head, we were already really good friends, hanging out at their local, with them insisting I went along to all their gigs.

This fantasy was inspired by him telling me about the time he'd been to Penzance with the Tremeloes on a Sunday night, for a gig that finished around midnight. He helped pack up the gear and then drove the van back to London. When they were on the outskirts of the capital, a Tremeloe took over the driving while Knotty climbed into the back and changed from his jeans and T-shirt into a suit. One of the country's biggest bands then dropped him off outside the offices of Hobson Bates and Partners just in time for work. No time for sleep, showering or breakfast.

This was a lifestyle that I craved, instead of the current one in which I went to bed early on a Sunday with a mug of Horlicks for a good night's sleep so as to leave me feeling fresh for the week ahead. I couldn't stop thinking about how thrilling and glamorous Knotty's life seemed. The Bromley win, which had seemed so exciting just a short time ago, was now all but forgotten.

When I got home, I headed straight to my record player and listened to both 'Yellow River' (paying particular attention to the drumming) and 'Silence is Golden' (listening out for the guitar), but something had changed. They sounded different now that I had a personal connection to both bands.

I was feeling good about life. Not only was I on the verge of becoming good friends with genuine pop stars but, for the first time since I'd started watching them, my football team were highly entertaining. They were no longer a one-man team, like they had been in the Stonebridge era, but a three- or four-man team. A team that could take us all the way to Wembley.

This feeling grew even stronger when I saw who Bromley had drawn for the next round of the FA Amateur Cup. Oxford City, who had famously gone nineteen games since their last win. I wasn't going to gloat if I got talking to any Oxford fans. I'd been through a similar run with Bromley and knew the feeling of helplessness.

Our opponents' winless streak was one of many encouraging signs going into the game. Another was that Bromley were now so good that nine of the team had been picked to play for Kent against Surrey in the Southern Counties Amateur Championship. Another was that one of the linesmen was called Charlie King.

And there were more favourable omens. Even in our worst-ever season, 1969/70, we'd beaten Oxford City in the FA Amateur Cup. And this season we'd been on the best FA Cup run I'd ever known, taking us past the Civil Service (10-0, with Slim Jim getting five and Coppin having to settle for three), Stevenage and Hayes, before a narrow loss to Guildford. Bromley had not travelled so far along the Wembley road for many seasons.

Mr Self tapped into the spirit of '49 in his programme notes, reminding us of then-captain Eric Fright's tannoy address to the fans before the first-round tie against Maidenhead, when he had famously said 'Give us your support and we'll bring home the bacon.' And bring home the bacon they did, winning the Amateur Cup on the first occasion it had been played at Wembley.

The current Bromley team had something else in common with the boys of '49. Both sides had to train using car headlights to illuminate the pitch. No one could remember why Eric Fright and Co. had had to do it, but the reason for the current arrangement was the power crisis, which was getting increasingly serious and had plunged the country into what seemed like permanent darkness.

As I read the programme, I came across a serious error when I saw that our captain, Roy Pettet, had had his name badly misspelled as 'Pettitt' in the team line-ups. This often happened in away games, when I had to fight the urge to inform the programme seller of the mistake, but Mr King, who was responsible for typing out the teams, really should have known better.

And it was Pettet who made the first contribution to the game, which was being played on a muddy and wet Hayes Lane pitch, on an overcast Saturday afternoon. He made a poor clearance, finding an Oxford City forward, who slipped the ball through for their top scorer, Eales, to add to his tally for the season. While it was a shock to find ourselves a goal down, it was more to do with the conditions than any uselessness on Pettet's part.

And while the conditions weren't helping Bromley, the same could be said of the referee, Mr A. C. Lines of Witham, Essex. He was useless, allowing his linesmen, one of whom hadn't even arrived on time, to run the game. The only time Mr Lines met with the crowd's approval was when he slipped over in the mud and ended up on his bum.

But despite this unfair disadvantage, Bromley's class eventually began to tell and when Alan Basham made a clever substitution, bringing the Welsh Wizard, winger Tony Nantcurvis, on, everything changed. Geoff Osborne, having what I considered to be his best game, tucked away the equaliser from close range at the second attempt to a collective sigh of relief from the Bromley fans around me. Normal service had been resumed and Bromley started playing the way they'd been playing for the past couple of months.

Oxford were visibly wilting and Osborne was clearly enjoying himself – on one run, he beat four men in the space of a telephone box before setting up Coppin, who headed narrowly wide. But then, with ten minutes to go, disaster struck. A cross from the left was glanced home by Eales for his second of the match and Oxford held on for a shock win, throwing me into a state of disbelief.

What had just happened? The last time I'd felt this way was when crawling from the wreckage of my Bond 875. Bromley had lost to Oxford City. How was that even possible? We were a million times better than them. The result made no sense. But, as Mr J. J. A. Bays of Leyton would have said, that is football.

After that disaster, I began to wonder which was the more likely scenario – getting a girlfriend or watching Bromley at Wembley?

The answer came the following season.

CHAPTER FOUR

When I looked ahead to the 1972/73 season, Wembley looked more like a certainty than a distant possibility. Following the loss to Oxford City the previous season, Bromley had shaken off the disappointment to embark on a run of barely believable results, culminating in the winning of the Kent Floodlit Cup (Western Section).

Crowds were on the up, optimism was sky high and life was good. I finally knew what it was like to support a successful football team – a team that had climbed from second from bottom in the Isthmian League to finish in eleventh place.

Even more impressively, it had been done without Slim Jim Brown, who had ruined my seventeenth birthday by announcing that he was leaving for Sutton. Sutton. As if I didn't hate them enough for beating us 9–0, they had now stolen our star player.

The credit for our upturn had gone to Alan Basham, Bromley's manager for the past three years, who looked like one of those black and white pictures you saw on the walls of barbers' shops – film-star features combined with heavily Brylcreemed hair. It was his intense fitness regime that was being held responsible. I wasn't convinced. Basham had used the same methods during the club's worst-ever season, when they had been blamed for our uselessness.

I often went along to watch training and take notes, and what I saw didn't fill me with confidence. One of the few pieces of exercise equipment was what looked like a car axle with uneven chunks of lead welded on to each end, which was being used as a lopsided makeshift barbell. It was hard to imagine players like Mick Channon or Ray Clemence being expected to do bench presses with one of these – apart from anything else, it would mean they'd have one bicep far bigger than the other.

I had no idea if Basham's methods actually worked, but I was happy to give them the benefit of the doubt – especially with the discovery that few things in life are better than a really strong end to a season. It sets you up nicely for the summer, when you can dream, with some justification, of great things ahead. The trouble was that, apart from those dreams, summer was boring – especially when there was no World Cup. I hated the thought of all those months sitting around in the sun, waiting for the new season to start.

But then Derek came to the rescue. He was organising a trip to the Norfolk Broads for a two-week holiday with a bunch of the Bromley coach regulars, including Peter, Roy and Davey. I felt a wave of excitement and anticipation no holiday had ever given me before. This was perfect – even if I couldn't watch Bromley, I'd be able to talk about them every day with people who felt the same way as I did. The only slight dampener came when I was told that Mrs Knott couldn't make it – I'd been hoping that he'd come, and bring his cousins with him.

This was my first holiday without my parents, and it got off to a bad start due to a misunderstanding over whether our boat already had a full tank, or whether we were meant to fill it before departing. Once onboard, Peter steered the boat towards Great Yarmouth at a steady five knots (we'd already taken to using nautical terms), when the engine suddenly cut out and we started to drift aimlessly, no one quite knowing what to do. Had we broken the boat already? Since no one volunteered to swim ashore, we had to wait for the boat to drift against the bank before someone (me) was sent to find a phone box and ring the people we'd rented the boat from. That was when we found out that we were supposed to have filled it up with petrol. As a result, someone (me) was despatched to find a garage. Luckily, I found one fairly nearby and they lent me a container to carry the petrol in.

After filling the tank, getting the boat working again and returning the container to the garage, we went in search of a pub. Several pints later (beer was 12p a pint, so a round was hugely expensive), we staggered back to the boat.

I liked being out in the country, miles from anywhere. Drifting off to sleep that night, with the boat gently rocking, I enjoyed the feeling of absolute peace and tranquillity. The silence of the still night air was broken only by the occasional shout of 'Come on Bromley!' from Roy, somewhere in the distance. He'd wandered off for a walk and no one quite knew where he'd gone.

By the next morning, he'd found his way home and we found a new pub, where much of the discussion revolved around our club, and it wasn't just me who was excited about the season ahead. Who wouldn't be excited by Coppin, Nantcurvis and Pettet? It really could be our year – not just with a chance to climb the league ladder, maybe even get into the top five, but in the Cup as well. Wembley was coming up more and more in conversations.

We also talked about the proposed changes to the Isthmian League. In a thrilling overhaul, the proposal was for it to be split into two divisions. A few Athenian League teams would be included, and promotion and relegation introduced. As Bromley were now a team that were unlikely to have to worry about dropping down, we were all excited by the idea.

When we got back to the boat, I decided to sunbathe. I lay on the deck, closed my eyes and reflected on how happy I felt being amongst friends, even though they were a bit more mature than me. I was forced to reassess this thought when I felt something hard hitting me on my forehead. Was it hailstones? Impossible in this weather. I opened my eyes and saw Roy and Derek, on the bank, giggling as they lobbed pineapple chunks (one of my favourite sweets) in my direction. All I could think was that Roy was showing more accuracy than I'd ever seen from him on a football field.

It was a new kind of holiday for me, one with friends and which was built entirely around beer and football. Apart from the pineapple chunks assault, and being thrown in the water by Davey, who was under the misguided impression that I was being an irritating teenager, it was one of the best times of my life. I loved being able to talk about football all day and to go to different pubs at lunchtime and in the evening. The only thing missing was girls. This was not a group of men that attracted a great deal of female attention and I'd pretty much given up hope of ever getting a girlfriend following a humiliating experience when asking The Grubby's sister out.

After several bottles of Whitbread Pale (one of the strongest beers around, according to a *Daily Mirror* survey), I plucked up the courage to ring her, knowing that she would be home alone. That was the brilliant thing I'd discovered about beer – it made it much easier to talk to girls, although I sometimes felt I wasn't talking much sense.

When Penny answered, I just came out with it. 'Hi, it's Dave, fancy going to watch a film sometime?' I asked. There was silence at the other end. 'Hello?' I said. Still nothing. After a couple more minutes of silence I heard the click of her putting the phone down. I found out afterwards that she didn't know how to turn me down.

But now, just a week after getting home from holiday and grudgingly returning to life as a suit-wearing civil servant, things were about to change. After another boring football-free Saturday, I went to a party being held by Bob, someone I'd gone to school with. Bob had been trying to fix me up with Mandy, his girlfriend's best friend. I'd been keen, but tried not to show it.

Mandy and I were both shy and stood in opposite corners, occasionally glancing at each other while pretending to have a good time. In the end, Bob had had enough and bundled us both into the dining room before locking the door. We had no choice but to talk to each other. Mandy wasn't that keen on football, but she loved Rod Stewart's 'You Wear it Well', as did I. Intriguingly, she lived just around the corner from the Crystal Palace ground, and half agreed to come and watch a game there with me sometime. I then asked her if she fancied going to watch a film sometime, which was my standard line. This time I got a 'yes'. When Bob let us out half an hour later, I had my first girlfriend.

This was turning into quite a year. I had a girlfriend. I also had a group of friends who I went on holiday with. And I had a football team poised on the cusp of glory. But one of the harsher lessons I'd already learned was that it is impossible for things to go well in every aspect of your life at the same time and that something always has to take a disastrous turn. In this case, it was football.

The first sign that Wembley may have been further away than I thought came with the first kick of the season, against Woking, when Colin Brown sliced the ball, only narrowly avoiding a spectacular own goal. The season went downhill from there.

By the end of August, we'd scored twice in five league games and had won none of them. In September, we won just one out of seven and, alarmingly, failed to beat Corinthian Casuals. October saw one win out of nine and the departure of star striker Tony Coppin. Then, leading up to the qualifying round of the FA Amateur Cup in November, I went to seven Bromley games in a row without seeing a single Bromley goal. SEVEN GAMES. That was 630 minutes without a goal. I began to curse my luck for having flu when we played Hayes at home and eighteen-year-old John Rains scored a goal in a 2-1 loss.

Why did Jim Brown and Tony Coppin have to leave? I still hadn't got over Alan Stonebridge's departure and it seemed that, every time Bromley had someone really good, they left the club for greener pastures.

I was getting really quite dejected by this point. I found myself looking far into the future, to the year 2010, when I'd be in my mid-fifties, and hopefully still with Mandy. We'd be sitting in our rocking chairs looking back at the good old days. Had I already lived through the high point? Would finishing eleventh in the Isthmian League be my fondest memory?

I still held out dreams of Wembley, but not based on anything rational, just blind hope. And when I saw that we'd drawn Harlow of the Athenian League at home in the qualification stage of the Amateur Cup, the normal reaction would have been joy at such an easy path into the first round proper. But these were not normal times – even if we'd drawn Park United, I wouldn't have felt confident.

Tony Coppin, who had left, and Roy Pettet were joint top scorers with three apiece from twenty-seven games. If Alan Basham had been given credit for the previous season, he had to take the blame for this. I wondered how he managed to keep his job. By rights he should have been sitting across a desk being interviewed by The Grubby, who now worked at the dole office. I was sure Basham couldn't survive much longer – especially since Bromley's honorary secretary, Charlie King, had just stated that the committee backed him 'to the full'.

Charlie King was an imposing and terrifying personality. What he said went. This season was his thirtieth with Bromley and, despite having only supported them for five years, I knew how thankless it could be. The club celebrated this anniversary (King's thirtieth, not my fifth) by buying a new clock and putting it at the top of the stand.

But Charlie was more concerned with the future than the past. The Isthmian League's proposal of expanding into two divisions with promotion and relegation had gone from being a good idea to one that directly threatened his club, which currently occupied bottom place in the upper tier. This may have been why Bromley, backed by Corinthian Casuals, were pushing for a different option, which made relegation impossible, yet somehow allowed for promotion.

The plan was almost impossibly complicated – something to do with splitting the league into two divisions, as proposed, but with the top three teams in each section playing off for the championship, the rest playing for a League Cup and clubs finishing first, third, fifth, seventh and so on going into one group and the rest going into another. It was the sort of overly complex system I used to fill my notebook with when I was fourteen, and I was encouraged to see Charlie confidently announce in the press that he was 'certain' it would be accepted – although this had become a more cautious 'almost certain' by the end of the article.

To the surprise of no one apart from our honorary secretary and me, the proposal was rejected, and the more logical promotion/relegation plan accepted. This seemed to push Charlie over the edge. He used the Harlow programme to lay into the local press, calling them 'dismal johnnies' who were 'preaching despondency and despair'. He criticised the supporters' club for not supplying 'heavy financial offerings', belittled Harlow for never having won the FA Amateur Cup 'whilst we had won it three times' and then, for good measure, attacked the few remaining Bromley fans for being too negative.

He went on to imply that being useless was an exciting indicator of things to come and was, in fact, a positive thing. 'On each occasion we have won the Cup,' he explained, 'the preceding seasons were as bad and disappointing as have been those we are presently undergoing.' He went on to add that 'optimists who are true supporters can gain hopes that their own club, even though it is having a bad run, may, in the not too distant future, once again be at the top.'

It was true that the supporters' club wasn't raising a great deal of money for the team. I knew from first-hand experience that we were selling very few pens and rosettes. Even sales of old programmes had slowed down to such an extent that the decision had been taken to reduce the price of many of them to either one or two pence, depending on their desirability. It was heartbreaking to have to write out the price stickers and I bought several myself, rather than see them virtually given away.

A long, dark cloud was hanging over the club and a win against Harlow was crucial. It would mean a windfall of nearly £150 for Bromley, which was much needed. And we started well, with Tony Nantcurvis, the Welsh Wizard, having a strong shot pushed around the corner by Howard in the Harlow goal. This signalled the start of a prolonged period of pressure and I started feeling confident of seeing a Bromley goal – my first in months.

But then a long ball found us exposed at the back. Phil Debnam failed to control a cross and Sedgewick nipped in to give the men in bright scarlet and white stripes the lead. The difference between the sides was spelled out when John Rains found himself in an identical position and fluffed the opportunity. Tony Coppin would have scored comfortably. I felt a familiar sinking feeling that no amount of tea and Battenberg cake could shake off.

Despite this, Bromley were comfortably on top in the second half. But then, after fifty-three minutes, something happened that was so hard to take that, for the first time I could remember, I wanted to leave before the end of the match. Rains curled in a beautiful cross, the defence panicked and the Harlow number four headed the ball against his own bar. From the rebound, Colin Payne headed the ball goalwards and, unbelievably, it thudded against the bar and fell into Howard's arms. When you hit the woodwork twice in three seconds, you know it's not going to be your day.

And so it proved. We were out of the Amateur Cup for another year.

At full-time, despite feeling totally crushed, I went and did my round of the bench end, collecting the used crockery. I'd noticed a new phenomenon that season. Occasionally, one or more of the teaspoons was bent, presumably by a bored spectator trying to do a Uri Geller and bend the spoon by rubbing it. I doubted very much that psychic powers were involved and was deeply disappointed to see this vandalism of club property, as I wasn't sure they could afford to keep replacing the spoons.

Another, more serious, act of vandalism had taken place after the game. Charlie King's Jaguar X 4.2 had been scratched all along one side and on the bonnet. Given his recent outbursts, the list of potential suspects must have been bigger than that in an Agatha Christie novel, but I was horrified. This was a man who devoted his life to Bromley FC, and who had led the team out at Wembley in 1949. These days, you'd often see the Jag parked outside a shop or billboard site, with an open pot of glue in the boot, as Mr King stuck posters up to advertise forthcoming Bromley fixtures. And you'd also frequently see him doing odd jobs around the ground.

I hoped they would catch whoever was responsible. Teams like Bromley needed people like Charlie King, even if they were a bit scary.

While we were losing to Harlow, the much-missed Tony Coppin was scoring twice to help his new team, Tooting and Mitcham, to a 4-2 win at Dulwich Hamlet and a place in the next round. This plunged me into new depths of misery. As did the naming of the Kent team. Last season, Bromley had provided nine players to the starting eleven. This season, only three were selected.

But if I thought Bromley had finally plumbed the depths, I was very much mistaken.

CHAPTER FIVE

1973 was a year of great change.

The Isthmian League had acquired a new name, added a second division and introduced promotion and relegation. Rothmans became the first sponsor of the league. It was also the beginning of the end of the amateur era, with the FA announcing a plan to make all teams either professional or semi-professional.

Most amateur clubs weren't remotely amateur, paying players by stuffing banknotes into their boots or by offering them jobs that didn't necessarily require them to turn up for work. Only Corinthian Casuals remained true to the spirit of the game and remained resolutely amateur, preferring to honour principles of fair play and sportsmanship. They usually finished bottom.

Players were now demanding – and getting – more money than ever before. Even Bromley's new groundsman decided he was worth more than the £21 a week he was on and walked out after his first few days. The professional era was well and truly underway.

Everything was changing, and that included me. I adopted a new image, which I was pretty sure made me irresistible to girls. The influence was Bryan Ferry from Roxy Music and I took to wearing a white suit with a bow tie and smoking Disque Bleu, which were pungent and very French, through a black ivory cigarette holder. I felt all of this gave me an air of sophistication which had been previously lacking in my life.

It wasn't long before I was forced to modify the new me, as I was banned from smoking Disque Bleu on supporters' club coaches: the smell caused loads of complaints and people refused to sit next to me. I wasn't too upset by the ban – Disque Bleu had an acrid taste that scalded the back of my throat and they smelled awful. I hated them and was happy to switch to Rothmans as a 'thank you' for their league sponsorship.

The Rothmans Isthmian League had also introduced three points for a win, in the belief that it would encourage attacking football by stopping teams settling for a draw. And, sure enough, Bromley scored fifteen in the first four games of the season, shared amongst our new, but lethal, strike force. Hardy, White and McDermid all hit hat-tricks during this time, which was testimony to the ability of Alan Basham to lure top talent. And, as if to prove the point, the great Jim Brown made a return following his brief spell at Sutton.

This Bromley team were so exciting to watch that I started turning up nearly two hours early for home games. As a result of this, I passed the time until the gates opened by watching bowls at the club next to the ground. I was soon hooked, although football would always be my main sport.

By the end of August, Bromley were third in the table and, if Basham had been offered a twenty-year contract, I wouldn't have objected. The only slight disappointment was that I'd had to stop wearing the suit and bow tie to matches. Despite its advantages, in terms of both style and practicality (programmes fitted perfectly in the inside pocket), I soon realised why more people didn't wear white suits to football. Apart from being openly laughed at, I had to get it dry-cleaned after every match as the bench I sat on was filthy. Bryan Ferry would never wear a dirty suit. Mind you, Ferry was unlikely to have got his from the Freemans catalogue and to have paid 75p a week for it over twelve months.

All in all, my reinvention as a style icon lasted about as long as Bromley's reinvention as a successful football team. I bought myself a bomber jacket and Bromley went the next ten games without a win.

My relationship status also changed around that time. Mandy and I split because we'd grown apart. At least that was what she told me, but I don't think either of us was particularly upset. Before we parted company, I'd managed to get her along to two carefully chosen Bromley home games – against Clapton and Corinthian Casuals – which at least proved to Roy, Derek and Peter that she existed, unlike her famed predecessor Paula. (I once described the fictional Paula to them as a pretty brunette with large brown eyes and a feather haircut, before

realising that I was describing Paula Wilcox, who starred in
ITV's *Man About the House*. Luckily, no one seemed to catch
on.)

I was between (real) girlfriends, so I decided to expand my
horizons beyond my friends' sisters. I moved on to fancying
my friends' sisters' friends. One in particular was Helen, a
friend of Dave's sister, Annie. And as Dave and I discussed ways
I could ask her out, a plan was slowly hatched. I liked it because
it showed (1) that I had wheels – I'd just bought a second-hand
Lambretta 175 scooter after borrowing £25 from my rich aunt
– and (2) that I was smooth and cool in a Bryan Ferry kind of
way.

The plan was simple. Dave would knock on her door and
then run away. As soon as he'd done this, he'd give a pre-
arranged signal, whereupon I would come around the corner
on my scooter in my white suit and bow tie and ride up the
path to her house before smoothly coming to a halt in front of
her.

Then I'd (smoothly) hand her the rose from my buttonhole
and, with raised eyebrow, say 'Fancy a ride?' At this point she'd
clamber onto the scooter, clutch me tightly around the waist
and we'd speed off to an olde worlde pub in Westerham which
I'd carefully chosen. It felt flawless. The kind of big, romantic
gesture that girls loved, if films were anything to go by.

Just to make sure, we held a dress rehearsal outside Dave's
house on the RAF base at Biggin Hill, which was identical to
Helen's house a few streets away. After driving up his path, I
added a nice touch – skidding sideways, which ended with me
stopping alongside Dave and handing him a red rose outside
his house. It worked perfectly.

By the time the day arrived, I was nervous but ready. As soon
as Dave gave the signal that he'd done his part and knocked on
her door, I revved up the engine, feeling the awesome power of

the Lambretta, and set off. Noticing that the speedometer had crept up to fifty, I slowed down and turned the corner as Dave scurried off. The last thing I needed was a disaster of Bond 875 proportions.

Helen was standing at the door, looking around. The plan had worked perfectly. With utter conviction that this was an idea of pure genius, I left the road and drove onto the path towards her. It was then that I saw a look on her face that was not one of swooning adoration, but one of fear and confusion. Suddenly, I saw things from her point of view. A young man she barely knew, wearing a white suit, bow tie and skull-and-crossbones crash helmet, was hurtling down her garden path towards her on a bright blue scooter. It suddenly seemed less like something out of a Hollywood romantic comedy and more like something out of a Hammer horror film.

She went back inside and slammed the door behind her. This deviation from the carefully planned scenario had thrown me and alarm swept through me. I was going too fast but, instead of using my right hand to brake, I panicked and twisted the accelerator, causing me to speed towards the spot where she'd been standing and, in swerving to avoid hitting the front door, I sped into the open garage, smashing into the bumper of her dad's much-loved, waxed and polished classic Rover 80.

The momentum sent me flying onto the concrete floor, which hit me flush on my nose, splattering blood over the white jacket. I lay there groaning in agony near where my scooter had landed, its wheels spinning wildly, oil gushing onto the floor.

I was vaguely aware of Helen coming into the garage to see what was going on. Through the throbbing pain I saw, with relief, that she had a look of concern on her face. At least it showed that she cared. Unfortunately, it wasn't me that she cared about.

'What,' she screamed, on the verge of hysteria, 'have you done to my dad's car?!'

By now Dave had joined us and, after checking the Rover, he explained that there was only a small scratch on the bumper. He then helped me to my feet and, between us, we picked the scooter off the floor and wheeled it out, before going back into the garage to clean up.

Although no bones were broken, the bruising was enough to keep me off work for four days. Miraculously, the scooter wasn't damaged beyond repair, unlike my romantic chances with Helen. But at least I still had football, even though it was another case of starting out full of promise and hope, before rapidly becoming a full-on disaster.

The perfect start to the season had led to a far more familiar pattern, and the build-up to the game against Boreham Wood in the fourth qualifying round of the FA Amateur Cup was less than ideal. After flirting with the top of the table in August, the next twenty-three games produced just two league wins, and one of them was against Corinthian Casuals. Which doesn't really count.

August's hero, Alan Basham, resigned after rejecting the club committee's offer of 'acting jointly with Eddie Firmani in charge of all team matters' and Firmani took over as sole manager. Which was probably the plan all along. Getting him was quite a coup, since most football fans – including me – had heard of him. He'd been capped several times by Italy when he was with Sampdoria and had also managed one of his former clubs, Charlton Athletic.

The training session on the Tuesday before the Boreham Wood game must have been quite a contrast from his playing days. Thanks to a combination of the petrol crisis (which meant few buses were running), train strikes and a player mutiny by Basham loyalists, only six of the squad turned up.

But Firmani wasn't put out. And he also seemed remarkably unaffected by the resignations of the last few remaining fan favourites: Roy Pettet was the biggest loss, with John Miles not far behind. The assistant manager, whose existence I was not aware of until then, also walked out.

A few days later came yet another blow when Firmani announced that John Knapman had returned to Walthamstow Avenue. But he felt that the future for Bromley was bright. He made a pledge to the fans that he would 'give them something to shout about' in the months ahead.

The *Bromley & Kentish Times* were less optimistic, although they did acknowledge that the new manager had plenty of ideas to 'make Bromley great again.' I loved this, as there was nothing I wanted more. I was getting increasingly nostalgic for an era from before I was born, when Bromley were a truly great team.

But before Firmani could deliver his ambition, the committee needed new faces – members with the business acumen to really get things moving. They needed to hurry, because our last-ever chance to win the Amateur Cup was only days away. With amateur football a thing of the past, it didn't make much sense to have an Amateur Cup. According to Mr Self, it would be replaced with the FA Trophy, which would be open to all teams outside the Football League.

Bromley had reached the first Amateur Cup final to be played at Wembley. It was unlikely that the current team would reach the last one to be played there. Unlikely, but not impossible. Especially with our new manager.

Despite the petrol shortage forcing the supporters' club to cancel the coach to Boreham Wood, I decided to queue for petrol early on the morning of the match. The last time I'd filled the Lambretta's tank at our local Esso garage it had only taken about half an hour to get a couple of hundred yards to the pump. And if I didn't have any luck there, I had a Plan B. My parents had bought a Flymo hover mower, after ignoring my recommendation of a Qualcast Concorde which was, according to the advert, 'a lot less bovver than a hover'.

This mower still had a full tank of two-stroke petrol from when the weather was warmer and the grass still needed cutting. My plan was to siphon it off through a plastic tube (I knew from experience that it tasted awful) and transfer it to my scooter. I wasn't 100 per cent sure that this would work, as I didn't really know what two-stroke petrol was, so my hopes were firmly pinned on Plan A.

As it turned out, the 'SORRY NO PETROL' signs were up at Esso, but Shell was open. Although it took well over an hour in a slow-moving queue to get to the forecourt, it was worth it. After filling the tank (which took less than the garage's limit of two gallons), I set off for Boreham Wood. This was a game I was confident of Bromley winning. Our opponents played in the Athenian League.

I'd rung around to see if anyone wanted a lift, but Roy, Derek and Peter all declined. I think it may have been partly because of what had happened in Helen's garage, and partly because it would have been illegal since I didn't have a full licence. They opted to try to get to the ground by train, which was a huge risk, because train drivers had embarked on 'a policy of non-co-operation' and a lot of trains were being cancelled.

It was a cold, wet, windy day. This was the worst thing about the early rounds of the Amateur Cup. The weather was always terrible. But it would be worth it if we reached Wembley six months later and I could watch my team in the warm May sunshine.

The weather played a big part in my decision not to wear the white suit. I'd seriously considered reviving it after seeing

Bryan Ferry on *Top of the Pops* a fortnight earlier, wearing his while singing 'Street Life'. He looked impossibly cool, but a combination of rain and the suit having a large tear on the elbow from my collision with Helen's garage floor was enough to convince me to wear the more practical bomber jacket.

It took me longer than planned to get to the ground as I spent much of the time driving through the backstreets of Borehamwood (the town was confusingly spelled differently from its football club), stopping every few minutes to check the *A-Z*. There can be few harder grounds to find than the one in Broughinge Road, especially when your team has never played there before. When I finally arrived, there was barely time to greet my fellow Bromley fans (whose train had got them there long before me) and buy myself a programme (a very reasonable 3p) before the match got underway at 2.15 p.m. Another victim of the floodlight ban.

It took about forty-five seconds for me to realise that I had underestimated Boreham Wood. That was how long it took them to open the scoring, when a free kick from the halfway line found Mickey Jackson, who headed the ball past Geoff Parsons into the Bromley goal.

We were standing right behind the goal, the wind and rain blowing directly into our faces, and had a perfect view of Alan Droy failing to pick up Jackson's run. I hadn't even had time to register the fact that Peter Deadman, one of my favourite players, was missing. I was told that he'd resigned a few days ago. Yet another one we were going to have to manage without.

But within a couple of minutes of conceding, Bromley were level and the long trip felt worthwhile. Jim Brown, the returning hero, took a shot from the edge of the area which seemed to be going wide until a defender deflected the ball past the keeper and it was 1-1. Wembley was still a distant possibility.

Boreham Wood were one of the dirtiest sides I'd seen all

season and free kicks seemed to be given against them constantly. My theory was that this unsettled the Bromley players,
which explained why, when Boreham Wood took the lead
again, it was another defensive mix-up. This time three Bromley defenders were involved. They were all staring at each
other to clear the danger from a corner, as Sneddon strolled in
to touch the ball over the line.

Boreham Wood's tea was as awful as Bromley's performance
and I wished I'd brought my Thermos flask. But there hadn't
been room in the scooter's storage compartment for that, my
sandwich box and the *A-Z*.

The wind grew even stronger in the second half and a Jim
Brown cross smacked against the bar to give a faint glimpse
of hope. But that was the closest we got. Not long after, the
home side's John Smith had a shot which Parsons seemed to
have covered, but it took a deflection off Colin Brown and
was diverted into the opposite side of the goal. It was identical to Bromley's equaliser, apart from the fact that our goal was
deserved and Boreham Wood's felt plain lucky.

The game fizzled out after that and, as I angrily navigated
the backstreets once again, I had plenty of time to contemplate
the events of the day. How could the team that had filled me
with such hope at the start of the season now fill me with such
rage? They had been terrible again, losing to a team from the
Athenian League. I thought about boycotting the next game
against Deal as a protest against the committee, but couldn't
bring myself to stay away. A lot of people did though. Hayes
Lane was virtually empty.

It was also a time of year when the bowls green was deserted,
so I missed one of the few remaining sources of pleasure at the
ground – my prematch ritual of watching the action at Bromley Town Bowling Club. At least I had the final of BBC2's *Top
Crown* to look forward to on Christmas Eve. Just to empha-

sise what a period of change this was, even the sedate world of bowls, my other love, was affected. Following in the footsteps of football, the word 'amateur' was removed from the tournament's name, allowing them to introduce a prize of £400.

At a time when the Isthmian League was introducing innovations like three points for a win, British Crown Green was introducing innovations like coloured bowls. Players complained bitterly – the reds were too heavy, the yellows too light and the blues had virtually no bias. But they soon got used to it, and it made for even more exciting TV. I looked forward to seeing the coloured bowls at my local club. I even thought about writing to the Rothmans Isthmian League to suggest coloured footballs, or even coloured boots.

In a year of dramatic changes, it seemed that one thing had stayed constant. Bromley were rubbish and I genuinely feared for the future. I no longer cared about Bromley being great again. I just wanted them to be average again. And with relegation now an option, I could see Bromley embarking on a downward spiral.

Eddie Firmani must have felt the same way because, nine weeks after he joined, he walked out following a 7-0 mauling at the hands of Leytonstone, leaving Danny Murphy as the third manager in as many months.

Yet again, I thought that things couldn't possibly get any worse for Bromley. Yet again, I was about to be proved horribly wrong.

CHAPTER SIX

If 1973 was the year of change, 1974 was the year of completely falling apart.

The first signs of my football world crumbling came that summer, with the World Cup, which was held in West Germany. Teams like Zaire, Haiti and even Scotland, with five Leeds United players, thirty-four-year-old Denis Law and an annoying song called 'Easy Easy', were there. England were not. For the first time in history we had failed to qualify, after losing 2-0 to Poland at Wembley, home of most of my dreams. I was forced to adopt a new team for the next month.

I had a soft spot for Zaire, because they were the Bromley of the tournament – even down to losing their second game 9-0. But in the end, I became a West Germany supporter. Apart from purely pragmatic reasons (I thought they'd win), I had a long-term German pen pal, whom I'd fancied since I had first met her on a school exchange visit to Mannheim a few years earlier. Her name was Petra, and she had sent me a World Cup T-shirt with a picture of a football and the word FUßBALL-WELTMEISTERSCHAFT on it, which I proudly wore with my Brutus brushed-denim flares.

I read far more into this gesture than was probably intended and immediately wrote back to thank her and ask her for a photo, using the barely credible or flattering excuse that I'd forgotten what she looked like. It wasn't my fault. When I'd met her, I was too scared to ask her to pose for a photo, so instead asked her to take one of me with her kid brother. This allowed me to think of her whenever I looked at it, as she was just feet away when it was taken. In the photo, I was squinting moodily into the distance, giving me a slightly dangerous yet devastatingly attractive look, modelled on Clint Eastwood in *For A Few Dollars More*, which I knew she liked. Sadly, the effect was ruined by her brother, sitting alongside me in his lederhosen, pulling a really stupid face.

In the same letter, I gushed about how great the West German team were. I loved it when people praised Bromley, so thought it would be a winning strategy. I told her about my admiration for goalkeeper Sepp Maier, using his nickname 'Die Katze von Anzing' to demonstrate how comfortable I was with the German language. I also raved about midfielder Günter Netzer and asked if she shared my astonishment that a player of his genius hadn't been picked for the opening game.

She wrote back a few weeks later – in English – to say that she hadn't been following the World Cup closely, but had every confidence that Herr Schön, the manager, knew what he was doing. More importantly, she enclosed a colour photo of herself standing under a tree in a yellow, sleeveless dress, looking quite serious. Her brown hair was a little longer than when I'd last seen her, and she had new glasses. Otherwise, she was exactly the way I remembered her.

The 1974 World Cup was enjoyable and impeccably organised. The Germans had even employed a computer to help them calculate when the weather conditions would be most favourable for playing fixtures, although this wasn't hugely successful, as a lot of the biggest games took place in torrential downpours. This included the hosts' decisive second group-stage match against Poland, when the kick-off was delayed because the pitch was waterlogged and the Frankfurt Fire Brigade had to be brought in to pump water from the sodden turf.

This can't have helped the nerves of Schön, who had already shown a fragile temperament when he had locked himself in his hotel room following a group-stage loss to East Germany. He refused to come out, even the next morning for breakfast and then lunch with his players. His press conference that afternoon was cancelled and he didn't reappear until the following day, still unable to speak.

Holland, on the other hand, were thoroughly enjoying themselves. Their team was packed with flair, from long-haired Johnny Rep to chain-smoking Johan Cruyff, and they had brought the concept of 'Total Football' to the tournament. This was a system in which every player had the skills to play anywhere on the pitch, in direct contrast to Bromley, where it could be argued that no player was skilful enough to play anywhere on the pitch.

The final between West Germany and Holland was OK, but the tournament just hadn't been the same without England there – although national pride was partially restored when Jack Taylor of Wolverhampton refereed the final.

It turned out that my only real hope of glory that year lay with Olivia Newton-John. She was representing the UK in the Eurovision Song Contest being held in Brighton, but her – and my – hopes were dashed by a Swedish group in glittery outfits and silver platform boots. The winning song, 'Waterloo', didn't even make sense. How can you feel like you win when you lose? That was garbage. I'd seen Bromley lose loads of times in recent years and it had never once felt like a win.

I was sure Olivia felt the same way. Despite clearly deserving to win, she could only manage fourth with 'Long Live Love'. Like most boys of my age, I fancied her – only Petra and Paula Wilcox were higher on my list of crushes – and I even helped her choose the song, in that I'd cast a postal vote for it using the official ballot form in the *Radio Times*.

My hopes for Bromley were a lot lower, especially since we wouldn't be playing Corinthian Casuals in the forthcoming season. They had, inevitably, finished bottom the previous season and been relegated – taking with them the only six points we could rely on.

The 1974/75 season in the Rothmans Isthmian League did not start well for Bromley. Leading up to our first-ever game in the new FA Trophy, away to Canterbury City, we lost ten league games in a row and Danny Murphy finally resigned. His record wasn't great, although he had briefly inspired headlines like 'MURPHY'S MARAUDERS' and 'DANNY'S DYNAMOS' when the team underwent a mini-revival consisting of one draw and one win. I couldn't see how a change of manager would make much difference with what was an awful squad.

One of the better players, John Bull, had resigned alongside Murphy and, since he'd actually scored a goal in his twelve appearances, was someone we could ill afford to be without. Inevitably, he scored twice on his debut for Clapton. Another five players, who were officially still with the club, hadn't been seen for at least a fortnight.

But the biggest loss was our captain, John Knapman. His first game for Walthamstow Avenue was against Bromley a few days before we went to Canterbury, so it was a foregone conclusion that he'd score – every time an ex-player plays against us, he will always score. It's just the way it is. And that's exactly what happened and we lost 3-1. Annoyingly, he hadn't scored for Bromley in almost a year. It took him thirty-five minutes to open his account for his new club.

As if Knapman's homecoming goal wasn't bad enough, the programme for the game had some terrible news. Our best player, and Knapman's successor as captain, John Rains, had been lured to Bishop's Stortford. It was a huge blow because he was solely responsible for keeping scores down to four goals or fewer in recent games. The only consolation was that he'd gone there and not to Sutton. I couldn't have taken him going to Sutton.

The *Bromley & Kentish Times* had an update a couple of days later. The programme notes were described as 'muddled' and Rains had, in fact, joined Sutton.

Bromley were in crisis. They were bottom of the league, players were walking out and the club had simply run out of money. The £1,000 raised from preseason advertising had all gone – and we were only three months into the season. Wages, or rather 'expenses' (professionalism had been put off for another year), had been cut in half and I was witnessing things that no football fan ever imagined they'd have to see. In the prematch kickabout against Tooting and Mitcham, Bromley had to use plastic footballs from Woolworths since, presumably, the budget didn't run to proper leather ones. What really hurt was the sight of Tooting players standing around laughing at my team as their practice shots were caught by the wind and floated slowly and harmlessly over the bar.

Then Mick Miles was forced to miss a couple of games because the heat-lamp treatment he was given for a muscle strain in his thigh turned out to have been given by a sun lamp and he ended up being rushed to hospital with a badly burned leg. Bromley's Medical Attendant probably left this episode off his CV.

The team were struggling so much that, in a London Senior Cup match against lowly Thames Poly, acting manager Bob Wright offered both of his tickets for Shirley Bassey at the Palladium to whoever scored the winning goal. Tony Davis duly obliged, although I'm not sure Mrs Wright would have been overly pleased when she found out she'd be missing the concert.

Players were banned from training on the pitch when it had rained. They were also banned from training on the pitch when it was frozen, as they were told that the club 'didn't want them breaking the grass.' And then there was the sight of Danny Murphy, in the last game before his resignation, being instructed by a committee member, during a match, to go and fetch the ball, which had been sliced out of the ground by a Bromley forward. There were no ballboys in the Rothmans Isthmian League.

I had felt a lot of things during my time watching Bromley – despair, hope, love, excitement, pride and pain. But this was the first time I'd felt embarrassed and humiliated. There seemed to be no end to the bad news – the next in a long series of depressing announcements came when the club revealed that Tony Davis (and his Shirley Bassey tickets) had joined the exodus away from Hayes Lane.

It was disaster after disaster. The team were barely recognisable – and barely up to Sunday League standard. And when the new manager, Tim Breen, was named just before the Canterbury game, it did nothing to inspire optimism.

His pedigree was several steps below that of ex-Italy international and Sampdoria star Eddie Firmani. Breen had formerly been in charge of Spartan League side Benstead Town and his main qualification for the job seemed to be that he lived in Catford, which was only about twenty-five minutes away on the 47 bus. His observation after watching the Walthamstow Avenue game was that 'not many players have the necessary skill for the Isthmian League.' I could have told him that for nothing.

What would the Bromley team of 1949 have made of all this? They had experienced all the highs that football can bring. The current side were the worst I had ever seen, which was saying something. There was no longer any pleasure in watching Bromley, only pain.

Crowds frequently dipped below a hundred. The local press had turned against the club, with the headline 'WHAT A JOKE' dominating the back page, above an article blaming the committee for making Bromley a laughing stock. Their priority seemed to be 'preparations to go professional', apparently unaware that the club were on the verge of falling apart. The only plan seemed to be that they would be taking 'actions yet to be finalised.'

It was too much for some. Apart from Roy, who never missed a game, and a few others, most of the old regulars had found better ways to spend their Saturday afternoons. Knotty, coincidentally, had decided to emigrate to South Africa. He joked that he was leaving because he couldn't take watching Bromley any more. At least, I think he was joking.

I was already looking at the *A-Z*, planning out routes to places like Ware Town, Finchley and Hampton, where we would be playing next season when we dropped down to the second division or, to call it by its proper name, the Isthmian League (Division 1). The only consolation – and it was a small one – was that we would once again be playing Corinthian Casuals. In normal times, this would have meant an automatic six points. But these were not normal times.

I didn't really want to go to Canterbury for the FA Trophy game. I was getting close to feeling that I couldn't carry on. What was the point? One of the joys of football – turning up without the slightest notion of how the ninety minutes would pan out – had been removed. Even the small glimmer of hope I'd had the previous season had gone. Watching Bromley, there was only one possible outcome. Defeat. Match after match I turned up to see my team lose.

I was now living in Neasden, sharing a house with some hippie friends of Dave, but somehow still found the strength to drag myself, with heavy feet, to the Underground station, to start the long journey to Canterbury, which involved a Tube, a train and then a long walk into a biting headwind and driving rain.

When I finally got to the Kingsmead Stadium, I bought a copy of the Canterbury Football Supporters' Club Official Handbook for 5p, to give myself something to read on the long journey back home. I also bought a programme and, if the articles inside were meant to intimidate opposition supporters, it worked. Canterbury seemed to have a stream of players who had gone on to greater things – Ian Christie was now with Coventry and had been called up by Don Revie for the England Youth squad. Mark Weatherly and David Wiltshire had made the Gillingham first team, while Pat Hilton was now a Blackburn regular. No wonder scouts from Chelsea and Spurs, amongst others, were regular visitors to Kingsmead.

This was only reinforced by their claim that, with footballs now costing £14 each, the club might be forced to sell more of their best players. They could always try plastic footballs.

The Bromley line-up required several names to be crossed out. John Rains had gone; John Mears was an unexplained absence although he was 'expected to resign'; while Andy Kalinka, one of the few bright spots in an otherwise dismal Bromley team, had broken his ankle on Tuesday.

Mick Miles, his burned leg fully recovered, was one of the few players worthy of wearing the Bromley shirt and was responsible for the few watchable moments, including a perfectly timed tackle to prevent Canterbury taking an early lead.

But there was a sense of relief amongst both sets of supporters when Canterbury's Alan Brown broke the deadlock with ten minutes to go. It was one of the worst games I'd ever seen, both teams packing their defences. It didn't really matter that we'd lost – neither team had the slightest hope of getting to Wembley.

Last season we had gone out to a team nicknamed the Lily-whites, like us. This season we had gone out to a team with three ravens on their badge, like us. I'm not sure anyone apart from me noticed, or even cared about, coincidences like this, but I felt that it was all part of an important pattern. The football gods had ordained it thus.

The Kingsmead ground had been built on a rubbish tip, which was apt given the rubbishness of both sides. I thought the *Bromley & Kentish Times* reporter was being overly generous when he described it as 'a scrappy bore totally devoid of originality and flair.'

But Kingsmead wasn't just a football ground – it was also home to the Canterbury Crusaders speedway team and an athletics track. I wonder if Charlie King had taken note of this because, less than a week later, he announced his ambitious one-man plan to rescue bottom-of-the-table Bromley FC from oblivion. His proposal was to sell about half of the club's land to the council and use a big chunk of the money to fulfil what he saw as the people of Bromley's greatest need.

He would build a large dance hall adjoining the ground. And when it wasn't being used for dancing, it could be used for wrestling, bingo, discotheques, judo and other indoor sports. Charlie's vision also included selling off the car park and building an underground car park beneath the dance hall. Other areas of land could be used for tennis courts, hockey and archery. Income from all this would be £20,000 a year – enough to 'restore our club to the higher sections of non-league football.'

For the first time in many months, I felt a stirring of hope. This seemed like a really good idea. And when you've scraped along at the bottom for so long, any hint of a way out is welcomed. I hoped the committee would back him. This was the kind of forward, ambitious thinking that Bromley needed, but the committee were not noted for forward, ambitious thinking. Their reaction was predictably cautious.

But the next week it was the turn of chairman Tom Ransom to put forward a plan, and his was even more radical. He wanted to sell off the ground completely and then lease it back. In a statement, he said, 'Unless something can be done swiftly we will dwindle to junior club level,' before adding, in a sentence unlikely to help the fragile confidence of the players, that 'Bromley is a big town and we should be worthy of a better team than at present.'

Both plans, of course, came to nothing. Within weeks, Tim

Breen had joined the ever-growing list of Bromley ex-managers, and the club appointed Len Wager, Charlie King's son-in-law, in his place. He did as well as could be expected but, by March, there was only a mathematical chance of avoiding relegation.

Our fate was sealed over a period of seventeen days that produced new depths of suffering. Wycombe Wanderers came to Hayes Lane and won 7-0 in front of a pathetic crowd. Just over a fortnight later, in the return fixture at Loakes Park, Wycombe won 8-0. The headline following that game, 'CURTAINS FOR BROMLEY', said it all.

There are times when it doesn't pay to take stock of your life, but that was what I found myself doing after relegation was finally confirmed. My football team were a complete disaster. The nearest thing I had to a girlfriend was my German pen pal, and I didn't know anyone else who still had a pen pal at nineteen. My job was rubbish – I was always getting told off and hated working in the civil service and filling out forms all day. I was living in a wreck of a house in Neasden with a bunch of hippies from Biggin Hill who didn't even have any furniture.

This was not how I had imagined my life turning out.

Someone who must have felt the same way was Charlie King. He was a decent man who had given thirty-four years of his life to his beloved Bromley FC, but he had now decided to announce his retirement. The last link to the 1949 side was now gone.

What Bromley needed, desperately, was a hero to rescue the club from completely falling apart. And just when he was needed most, a hero duly arrived.

CHAPTER SEVEN

Taking stock of my life in late 1976 was a lot more satisfying a process than it had been two years earlier. For starters, I had moved to Grove, a small village near Oxford, with Dave and one of his non-hippie friends. The best feature of the house was a second-hand three-piece suite, which represented a significant lifestyle upgrade on the living room in Neasden. That had contained two worn deckchairs, a beanbag and a multi-purpose half brick, which was used as both a communal ashtray and, thanks to the holes in it, as a joss-stick holder.

We also now had the luxury of curtains, instead of a huge Soviet flag permanently taped over the bay window, which had kept the smell of stale cigarette smoke in and the daylight out. More importantly, we had an off-licence less than eighty yards away. I regularly bought a bottle of Dubonnet there, the last remaining affectation from my Bryan Ferry era.

But apart from the improvement in living standards, I had plenty to celebrate. The year had started brilliantly when a referee from Great Bookham had booked eight players in the Bromley v Horsham game. Then Bromley found the hero it so desperately needed, in the burly shape of new manager John Biddle. A tough, uncompromising leader of men, and one sporting an impressive moustache, Biddle had formed a plan to save the club which was a lot more effective than all the other plans put together.

His idea – so radical that I could scarcely have thought of it myself – was to get rid of all the useless players and replace them with really good players, mostly from his previous club, Cray Wanderers. It worked brilliantly. Biddle brought in John Duffy, a big bruiser of a striker who combined with the impossibly cool Junior Crooks (with his Afro and untucked shirt) to form a partnership which seemingly scored at will. Other key signings were the midfield partnership of Phil Maw and Derek Brown, who were several levels above anything we'd seen before. The change in personnel coincided with the club's decision to become semi-professional, and Bromley's first player to officially be paid was David Mann, a tree surgeon from Penge.

Things were also looking up for the country as a whole, as Brotherhood of Man restored national pride by winning the Eurovision Song Contest with 'Save Your Kisses for Me'. I had uncovered a link between the UK's performance in the Eurovision Song Contest and Bromley's performance in the Rothmans Isthmian League. However, Eurovision was something I no longer watched, or at least admitted to watching. Because I had recently become a punk rocker. This meant having to walk around with a permanent sneer on my face (which I often forgot to do) and wearing a bin liner with torn jeans.

It was unclear where punks stood on football, but Dave, who was now a fellow punk, managed to convince me that Johnny Rotten, who grew up near Highbury, was a lifelong Arsenal fan (this turned out, in fact, to be true). Since another notable punk, Siouxsie Sioux, had grown up in Bromley, there had to be an admittedly slim chance that she might be a Bromley fan – although I was fairly certain I hadn't seen her, or any of her

Banshees, at Hayes Lane, since she would have been hard to miss.

But despite the distant possibility of seeing Siouxsie in a black and white scarf, I decided against going to watch Bromley play lowly Medway from the Kent League in the preliminary round of the FA Trophy. There seemed little point, as experience told me that Bromley would fall at the first hurdle, like they always did. I had no confidence whatsoever, despite the odds being loaded in our favour – we played several levels higher and, if there was a draw, the replay would also be at Hayes Lane as Medway didn't have floodlights. None of this mattered, since we had never, ever won an FA Trophy game.

In the event, Bromley comfortably won 3-0, with goals scored by Bobby Adams and Derek Brown (2). I'd arranged for a programme to be sent to me, from which I learned that the match ball had been donated by Mrs M. Ransom, the chairman's wife. My regret was not in missing the win, but in missing a game in which the Bromley goalscorers' surnames began with A and B, while the referee's surname began with A and the linesmen's surnames began with B and C. I was fairly certain that this was history-making, but couldn't prove it and, besides, no one I told seemed interested.

The draw for the first qualifying round saw my worst nightmare come true – we would be playing Carshalton, the only team I hated more than Sutton. Carshalton. The club who had lured Alan Stonebridge away when I was thirteen, delivering a blow from which I felt I would never be able to recover. Bromley went into the game having lost only twice in their last seventeen games. Both losses were to Carshalton. No wonder I hated them.

I couldn't bear the thought of seeing them rub it in as they put us out of the Trophy, so stayed at home. The result, when I saw it, had me staring at the *Observer*'s football pages in disbelief. An injury-time goal from John Duffy had given us a 2-1 win, and for the first time we were through to the second qualifying round, where we faced a trip to Folkestone and Shepway of the Southern League.

A week after beating Carshalton, we beat Walton & Hersham 9-3 in the FA Cup, with Smash (John Duffy) and Grab (Junior Crooks) scoring five between them. Bromley had entered Optimum Bromley phase, the purplest of purple patches. Biddle's Battlers, as the *Bromley Advertiser* so rightly called them, were playing breathtaking football.

And a fortnight later came the most glorious performance of all. We lost 7-0 at Third Division Swindon Town. While the result itself wasn't overly impressive, the performance was. It would have been a really close game if it hadn't been for six late goals, which were scored after Bromley simply ran out of steam. At least it saved John Biddle from having to walk home down the motorway, which is what he had threatened to do if Bromley won.

Going to Swindon and watching a settled Bromley team who were actually good, as well as seeing Roy, Derek and Peter again, had reawoken something in me. Although moving to Grove had meant fewer visits to Hayes Lane, the obsession, ground down to dust through years of abysmal football, had returned to its former dimensions. Seeing Wembley as a real possibility, I begged Dave to give me a lift down to Folkestone, as I didn't fancy the mix of bus, Tube and trains. Dave had bought himself a highly distinctive lime-green Mini. The colour was so hideous that he had demanded, and got, £50 off the asking price because of it. The only upside was that it was easy to find in a car park.

When you share a house, bribery and negotiation play a big part in daily life. Eventually, it was agreed that Dave would drive me down to the game (and to any subsequent replay or replays) and, in exchange, I would clean the Mini inside and out, make him eggs on toast for breakfast for a week and also clean and polish his cowboy boots – which I felt was ridiculous, as he'd stopped wearing them since becoming a punk. I would also have to pay for the petrol.

I hadn't felt so excited about football since I had first started watching Bromley, so when I saw in the *Radio Times* that a film about football was showing on BBC2 a few nights before the Folkestone game, I had to beg my housemates to let me watch it and, as both liked football, succeeded in doing so. It turned out that the film, *Football of the Good Old Days*, was a subtitled Hungarian comedy which wasn't remotely funny but, since I'd made such a fuss about watching it, I had to sit through the whole thing laughing and pretending to enjoy it.

Dave had made a punk-rock cassette for the journey to Folkestone, which consisted of all three punk records that we owned between us – 'I'm Stranded' by the Saints, 'New Rose' by the Damned and 'Anarchy in the UK' by the Sex Pistols. It did get a bit repetitive, but since the only other cassette he had was the soundtrack to the musical *South Pacific*, which he'd become obsessed with since finding it at the Oxfam shop, I didn't mind.

As we made our way down the M4, heavy rain bounced off the tarmac, which just a few months earlier had been melting due to the extreme heat. The summer of 1976 was the hottest I'd ever known and this brought with it a new insect threat. As if wasps weren't bad enough, I now had to worry about being attacked by ladybirds. They were everywhere, swarms of them, and since there was nothing left for them to eat (all the plants had died in the drought), they turned on humans, trying to rehydrate by drinking people's sweat. The river running along the back of our house in Grove was covered in psychotic, thirsty ladybirds.

Despite this, Dave and I spent a lot of time playing football in the garden. And after watching all four games in the European Championships, one incident had a huge influence on our kickabouts. Antonin Panenka's penalty for Czechoslovakia in the final against West Germany, when he audaciously chipped the ball straight down the middle as Sepp Maier dived to the left, changed the game for ever. Within hours we were taking penalties against each other, but the craze didn't last long. We soon worked out that whoever was in goal simply had to stand still and catch the ball.

The hot, dry weather was so relentless that, when I went along to watch some action at the Wantage Bowling Club, the greens were so dry that they'd turned a brownish yellow with a network of cracks, making them unplayable.

But it was now December, and the only heat came from the fan heater built into the dashboard, which was blasting hot air, dust and the smell of petrol into our faces.

Somehow, despite the limited visibility, Dave found his way to the Cheriton Road ground and there was an unexpected surprise awaiting us. The programmes were free, with the compliments of their advertisers. If this was the future, I was all for it – Bromley still charged 5p.

The advertisers, as usual, made every attempt to tie themselves to football. An estate agent asked: 'Is your GOAL to KICK OFF with a new HOME?'; a tobacconist said that 'Everyone likes to see a good STRIKER in action – is your cigarette lighter efficient?'; while the local Ford dealer claimed to be 'Always on the BALL'.

Folkestone started the game as they meant to go on. Just a few minutes into the game, a terrible tackle from their big striker left Junior Crooks writhing around in agony. He was carried off and, despite trying to come back onto the field, was replaced just after half-time. Folkestone were a dirty, niggly side and the whistle of Mr Smith (Margate) frequently brought play to a halt.

It was typical of the unfairness of football when Housden, the striker who had chopped Junior Crooks down, put the home side ahead with a low drive. But Bromley drew level when Neil Cugley, who had just been booked for a vicious foul on Paul Maw, sent Paul McCarthy sprawling in the box and Alan Hawkins equalised from the spot. A draw was a good result, especially since Dave was legally obliged to drive us down to Hayes Lane for the replay on Tuesday night without my having to do any further jobs for him.

When the time came, I was expecting protests but, surprisingly, he didn't seem to mind. He'd been sufficiently impressed by the performance at Folkestone to become a temporary Bromley supporter.

The rain, which hadn't stopped for several days, was still pouring down when we left home. It was only a two-and-a-half-hour journey but tiredness, combined with listening to the same songs over and over again, made it feel longer. We'd both been up since six, as we both worked for British Leyland, although in different factories.

When we arrived at Hayes Lane at around 7.15 p.m., the rain, if anything, had got even worse. And as Dave steered his lime-green monstrosity past the bowls club and into the car park, something occurred to us. There were no other cars, the floodlights hadn't been turned on and we hadn't driven past a single spectator. When we got to the gate, we found out why. A large strip of paper saying 'POSTPONED' had been pasted over the poster advertising the game. Underneath, someone (presumably a committee member) had scrawled 'To be played THURSDAY weather permitting'.

There can be nothing more depressing than standing in the freezing rain after a wasted two-and-a-half-hour drive, with just a bin liner held together with safety pins and a parka to protect you from the elements, and finding out that there would be no football, tea or Battenberg cake.

We immediately blamed each other for not ringing ahead to see if the game was still on, and the journey back was carried out mainly in silence, broken only when Dave stopped to fill up at the motorway services and demanded petrol money. The only good thing to come out of the whole episode was that Junior Crooks had another few days to recover. As did we.

I didn't sleep well on the night of the replay, a combination of excitement about the game and adrenaline running through me after seeing the Sex Pistols swearing at Bill Grundy on TV. At work the next day, I felt a surge of pride as I saw the headline in the *Daily Mirror*, which was the paper of choice for most of my fellow British Leyland workers. 'THE FILTH AND THE FURY,' it screamed. Below were articles entitled 'UPROAR AS VIEWERS JAM PHONES' and 'WHO ARE THESE PUNKS?' Little did they know that a real punk was amongst them. I couldn't reveal this as, judging by the comments flying around that morning, I probably would have got beaten up.

By the time I got home, the rain had started to ease. I changed out of my overalls and into my bin liner with more pride than usual. Dave, experiencing similar emotions, wore his red T-shirt with the words 'I don't care' painted on it in white paint. Before setting off, we made sure the game was definitely on by ringing the club and the news was good. There was no doubt that it would be going ahead.

Halfway through the journey, the recent lack of sleep started catching up with me, but once we got to Hayes Lane, tiredness was soon forgotten. Especially when Paul Maw put Bromley ahead with just twenty minutes left. Just as I was starting to look forward to the next round, where the winners would face

Hastings, Westgarth grabbed a late equaliser against the run of play. This meant half an hour of extra time, which meant another late night. And when extra time failed to break the deadlock, it was announced that there would be yet another replay, this time on Monday at Hayes Lane.

Our enthusiasm was definitely being tested. We were both getting fed up with the long drive and with each other. Both of us started work early, and the late nights driving to and from football were taking their toll. Dave insisted on playing the *South Pacific* soundtrack endlessly, just to annoy me. Everything about him was starting to annoy me, from his stupid haircut to his insistence on loudly singing along to 'There is Nothin' Like a Dame'. I didn't want to give him the satisfaction of knowing he was getting to me, so I kept the rage inside. Seven years of watching Bromley teaches you how to do that.

When we arrived at Hayes Lane once again on the Monday, the weather seemed to have had an effect on the crowd, which was sparse. The ground was waterlogged and both goalmouths were so muddy that it was hard to make out the penalty spots.

The conditions got even worse when a torrential downpour occurred after twenty minutes. There was a serious danger of the game being abandoned, which would have meant yet another trip, but the rain eventually stopped. By then, Bromley were in complete control and it only seemed a matter of time before they scored. The Folkestone keeper, Boorman, was having an incredible game, making impossible saves firstly from Maw and then from McCarthy, when he clawed the ball out from under the bar and away for a corner.

While relieved that we had weathered the storm without the match being abandoned, there remained the possibility of Folkestone, thanks to their goalkeeper, holding out for a draw. Which would mean the unthinkable prospect of yet another replay. If this was to be Bromley's Wembley year, it would be a long, long road getting there.

Extra time inevitably arrived and, when a further half hour passed without a goal and time was up on the clock, the scores were still level. Dave and I looked at each other, wearily. Were we really going to have to go through all this again? But another replay would have been infinitely preferable to what happened next. In the dying seconds of extra time, Housden (who else?) rammed a ferocious header past Malcolm Broadway and Bromley were out of the FA Trophy, after five and a half hours.

Tiredness only made the disappointment worse and the journey back to Grove seemed to go on forever. But I knew from experience I'd soon get over it. The next day, enthusiasm fully restored, I decided that I'd go to every Bromley game in the following season's FA Trophy, even if I had to walk down the motorway to get there. Which would probably have been preferable to having to sit in a car with Dave for hours on end.

I didn't care who we played. Just as long as it wasn't Folkestone and Shepway.

CHAPTER EIGHT

Throughout the 1970s, Bromley's clubhouse became a magnet for unambitious criminals. A series of late-night break-ins resulted in the vandalism of the honorary secretary's adding machine, followed by the theft of a wooden plaque and a clock that was due to be taken in for repair.

The crime wave reached its zenith in 1977, when a perfectly executed heist relieved the club's fridge of an opened packet of sliced ham and a quarter of a pound of mild cheddar. It was called 'The Great Sandwich Robbery' in the papers, but that was giving the thieves more credit than they deserved, since no bread or butter was taken.

But while local wrong'uns were enjoying limited success at Hayes Lane, the team were exceeding all expectations. John Biddle had brought a winning mentality to the club. He had also brought Junior Crooks with him, who had soon become my favourite player, as well as the coolest person I had ever seen in the flesh.

Despite not reaching Wembley that year, Bromley did manage the next best thing: a trip to Maidstone Stadium for the Kent Senior Cup final, where we played Gravesend and Northfleet. On a mudbath of a pitch on a chilly late April afternoon, Crooks (who else?) scored the only goal of the game with a rifled left-foot drive from the edge of the area, and Bromley had won. The hundreds of supporters who had made the short journey went wild, running onto the pitch and mobbing their heroes.

No cup was bigger than the Kent Senior Cup, in the sense that it was at least double the size of any other trophy I'd cast my eyes upon. Skipper Dave Mann did well to hoist it above his head and looked relieved when he passed it over to Phil Emblem.

This was the best Bromley team I'd ever seen, and the future had never looked brighter. I couldn't wait for August and the start of the new season.

But before then, in the absence of any football, the highlight of the calendar was the Queen's Silver Jubilee celebrations. As a punk, I viewed the royal family in the same way that I viewed ABBA, in that being a punk meant I had to publicly hate them, but I secretly liked them.

As luck would have it, I was never forced to choose between punk and royalty, as my punk days came to a sudden and unexpected end less than a fortnight before the Jubilee. One evening, I'd gone to the off-licence for a bottle of cider (which had replaced Dubonnet on the grounds that it was cheaper) and come home with a black eye.

The assault, by a couple of farming types I'd seen around, may have been because of my punk outfit (Johnny Rotten was beaten up regularly), or it may have been prompted by having SOD THE JUBILEE – a line I'd got from a Clash song – painted on my bin liner. I never did find out.

But getting attacked was the final straw after being threatened at least once a week. It was the end for both Mucus Membrane (my punk name, which never really caught on) and the bin liner (which was crumpled up and thrown into the bin liner hanging from the kitchen door handle). In all honesty, I wasn't going to miss wearing it. What no one tells you when you become a punk is that, in hot weather, which we were then experiencing, a bin liner is incredibly uncomfortable and sticky.

Despite leaving me sore and feeling sorry for myself, the punch wasn't the most memorable one I'd see all year – that would come later. And my new, post-punk look was unlikely to offend anyone. I took to wearing a plain T-shirt with rainbow braces (as worn by Mork on ITV's *Mork and Mindy*) underneath an oversized brown cardigan with baggy jeans. It was far more suitable for the Silver Jubilee.

The nearest large town to Grove was Wantage, where the Jubilee celebrations took place in the market square. There was bunting everywhere, a band playing and a massive crowd of people drinking, wearing straw hats and waving Union Jack flags.

Dave, Gary (an occasional housemate) and I embarked on a Wantage-wide pub crawl and, while we were enjoying a pint at the fifth or sixth stopping point, Gary decided it would be a good idea to offer me £5 to streak around the market square. I declined his offer, horrified at the thought. Who did he think I was? When he raised it to £10 and Dave offered to match it, I nodded my acceptance. Every man has his price.

And that was why I found myself getting undressed in the toilets of the King Alfred's Head. I wasn't sure about streaking protocol. Does a streak start in the pub, or when you get outside? Since walking through a crowded pub naked didn't appeal, I sprinted through the bar and out of the door.

The glare of daylight temporarily blinded me, but my eyes soon adjusted. When I saw that the square was packed and that quite a few people had already noticed me, I felt a wave of terror. I'd heard that alcohol can cloud judgement, and I wondered if the six pints I'd drunk that afternoon had influenced my decision.

But the fear soon turned into exhilaration. I was running faster and faster and felt like Billy Whizz from the *Beano*, the fastest boy in the world, who was so quick that he avoided raindrops and whose stopwatch was too slow to time him. As soon as people registered what was happening, I was gone.

By the time I got to the final bend, the end was in sight and two tenners would be mine. But then a tendency of mine, which had begun with the Bond three-wheeler, came back to haunt me, with disastrous consequences. I took the corner too fast, rolled my ankle and felt searing pain shoot through me.

My foot was already swelling up as I limped the tantalising last twenty or thirty yards to the King Alfred's Head, a large crowd watching my every painful, naked step. Sensing a way to avoid paying out if I didn't finish the dare, Dave and Gary refused to help. It must have taken no more than two minutes to get there, even though it felt more like two hours.

While I was hobbling, I kept a wary eye out for the farmer types who had given me a black eye. If they were offended by a bin liner, I couldn't imagine they'd look upon public nudity any more favourably. When I finally reached the public bar, Dave and Gary reluctantly handed over the money, and I grabbed it despite having nowhere to put it.

Had it been worth the entire population of Wantage and the surrounding areas seeing me naked? Probably not. But that couldn't detract from what had been a great day.

And just when I thought being British couldn't be any better, Virginia Wade won Wimbledon, beating Betty Stove in the final. The feelgood factor then continued into the football season, when Bromley were unbeaten for their first five games, winning four of them.

I was able to stay in touch with my team's progress thanks to my mum sending me the *Bromley & Kentish Times* every week. It arrived on Saturday morning, which was the perfect time to read the preview of that afternoon's game. And that was how I found out the FA Trophy draw, a week later than anyone else. I was desperately hoping we'd get Workington at home, since they'd just been kicked out of the Football League and were still a big club. In my eyes, anyway.

We didn't get Workington at home, but at least we didn't get Folkestone and Shepway again. Instead, it was another team that had recently beaten us in the Trophy, Canterbury City. This time, however, we were far better prepared. This time we had Junior Crooks and John Duffy.

And at the beginning of September, we duly took revenge on Canterbury, by winning 3-1, with two goals from Crooks and one from Duffy. At this stage of the Trophy in the previous season, the goalscorers' surnames had begun with A and B.

This season, the goalscorers' surnames began with C and D. Did this mean anything? Probably not. But as I said, it seemed important.

By the end of September, we were second in the league, which opened up a whole new source of anxiety. It was easy supporting Bromley when they were rubbish. When you're mid-table or lower, a win is good, but so is a draw. Losing is depressing, but never unexpected. But now, if we didn't get the full three points, it would take days, even weeks, for me to get over it.

I was looking forward to the draw for the next round of the FA Trophy. There were more than sixty teams we could have been paired with and I studied the list to pick out my preferred opponents. I got it down to Southall & Ealing Borough, Gorleston or Witney Town – the first two because I'd never heard of them and the third because it was a bus ride away from Grove.

But none of these names came out of the hat. Folkestone and Shepway were still in the competition, so obviously we drew them. Again. I didn't even bother trying to bribe Dave to take me, knowing that his demands would be beyond unreasonable. I'd have to make my own way down to Bromley. I just hoped Folkestone weren't going to be as dirty as they had been the previous year. The last thing we needed was a run of injuries.

As I left for Hayes Lane, Dave asked why I was going all that way just to watch a draw. As usual he was wrong. This wasn't the Bromley he'd seen; this was the high-flying, all-conquering Bromley, who were second in the Isthmian League (Division 1).

When I got to the ground, and opened the programme, I found that the new honorary secretary, John Cooper, was carrying on where the old one had left off, by weaving frequent complaints about Bromley fans into the club news. After boasting that the jackpot had twice reached new heights in recent weeks, with winners pocketing £11, he complained that this had brought problems in the form of spectators tearing up non-winning tickets and throwing them on the ground along with sweet papers. He pointed out that having to pick them up was 'a back aching job for those whose job it is to clear up after matches.'

The crowd was low, perhaps because the novelty of watching Folkestone had worn thin, and the game soon took on a familiar pattern of vicious tackling and niggly fouls. I was impressed with Bromley's discipline, despite huge provocation. Once again, Folkestone seemed to be targeting Junior Crooks and, within minutes, one of his socks had been torn to ribbons by an opponent's studs. They were the dirtiest team I'd ever seen, even worse than anything I'd come across in the Orpington and District Sunday League.

Not long after their worst offender, Neil Cugley, was booked after kicking Derek Brown, Folkestone took the lead through Keith Robinson but, ten minutes later, Brian West equalised from close range following a free kick given away by Cugley.

Then Malcolm Broadway, who had won £5 in the '200 Club' weekly draw, continued his good week by making one of the saves of the season from a Westgarth drive. Inevitably, the match finished 1-1 and it was announced that the replay would take place at Folkestone on Wednesday.

But it was another announcement immediately afterwards that got my attention. The club were holding a disco that night, so I hung around and passed the time by picking up jackpot tickets, sweet papers and, unforgivably, carelessly discarded programmes. What was wrong with people?

Then it was disco time.

I wasn't sure what to expect, although I clung on to a million-to-one chance of meeting an Olivia Newton-John looka-like, obsessed with Alan Stonebridge and Junior Crooks, who was desperate to find a socially awkward ex-punk who worked in a car factory.

The first signs were encouraging. There were quite a few girls, although none quite matched my requirements, and it looked like a proper disco – as opposed to a non-league team's clubhouse where frequent low-grade crimes had taken place. There were coloured lights attached to the ceiling and the DJ (Charlie King's grandson) had professional-looking sound equipment.

There were the usual groups you saw at every disco. The girls, dancing in a line, handbags on the floor. The boys, against the wall, staring longingly. A few couples snogging. But on this occasion, there was another, less predictable sight.

A young man, around my age, was pogoing with uncon-fined joy, throwing himself around with complete abandon to the distinctly non-punk 'The Name of the Game' by ABBA. He was totally caught up in the moment and had a wide grin on his face.

I found out that he was known as either Pogo Pete or Peter the Punk, which, as names went, I felt were a step or two down from Mucus Membrane, but I loved his lack of self-conscious-ness. Punks may have worn a T-shirt saying that they didn't care, but Peter the Punk showed it in the way he acted. It was many years later that I found out that he was Roy's brother.

After about half an hour of standing around trying to look indifferent, I left. Alone. I wasn't really in the mood, still stung by drawing a game we deserved to win and by the unfair treat-ment dished out to Bromley's players. And the fact that no girls had come up to me and started chatting me up.

When I got back to Grove, there was further disappoint-ment. Dave told me that Italy had put six past Finland in their

World Cup qualifier, which made England's task a lot harder. They would need a huge win at Wembley later in the year to book their place in Argentina.

In my down time at work the following Monday, I took my notebook and planned tactics for the Trophy replay a couple of days later. I felt I'd seen Folkestone enough to know their game strategy, which was basically to kick our best players, tackle them from behind, punch them when the ref wasn't looking and freely use their elbows.

It was a long journey to Folkestone, and I had to take the afternoon off, but I was sure it would be worth it. When I arrived, it was good to see a couple of fellow Bromley fans walking to the ground. They were both in their teens and were wearing white Bromley shirts, with the three stripes on the left at the front and the ravens badge on the right. I was immediately filled with jealousy. I'd never seen them in the shops and never seen any other fans wearing them. I wanted one. But where had they got them?

Under questioning, they admitted that they had bought Manchester United away shirts from Debenhams, which were almost identical, and then bought badges from the Bromley club shop, which their mums had sewn over the United badges. It was ingenious. But I didn't trust my own sewing and, at twenty-two, I felt I might be a little old to ask my mum, so reluctantly decided to wait until real Bromley shirts went on sale at the club shop.

When we arrived at Cheriton Road, the joy of getting a free programme turned to disbelief when I started reading it. The club secretary (who doubled as vice-chairman) was complaining about another team, Sheppey, using dirty tactics in a Kent Senior Shield game.

'I do feel, very strongly,' he thundered, 'that players are entitled to better protection from referees for persistent tackling from behind when in possession of the ball, certainly more than they received in this match.'

Then the irony meter exploded.

'Under no circumstances do I condone retaliation by a player, but I do understand that it takes superhuman self control to remain calm after continuously being brought down.'

I had to read it twice. Were Folkestone, the dirtiest team I had ever seen, seriously complaining about foul play?

I was still in shock about this as the teams took the field for what seemed the hundredth time in the last twelve months, and Folkestone were soon up to their usual tricks. Paul McCarthy was sent sprawling after a crude challenge from behind by Neil Cugley, who was responsible for at least 75 per cent of his side's more serious assaults.

Bromley, meanwhile, concentrated on football and took the lead through a near-post header from Brian West. This was the cue for Folkestone to get even more physical and, by half-time, they had bludgeoned their way to a 2-1 lead. The dressing room must have resembled a casualty ward during the interval, as Phil Emblem, Crooks and McCarthy all needed patching up.

To no one's surprise, it wasn't long before Folkestone were down to ten men, following a high tackle by the previously booked Westgarth on Keith Bradbrook.

Bromley soon took advantage and equalised through a determined run and tidy finish from Phil Emblem. The atmosphere was red hot and I felt a strange mix of fear and excitement, with the feeling that things could explode at any moment.

And then they did.

John Duffy, who would never be described as 'even-tempered', finally snapped when he saw Cugley viciously – and blatantly – kicking goalkeeper Malcolm Broadway in the face, while he was on the ground clutching the ball. Duffy, fuming, marched half the length of the field up to the big number five, his path clearing like the parting of the Red Sea, and laid him out flat with a right hook. He then began to march towards the changing room, without glancing at the referee, and disappeared down the tunnel. It was the first time I'd ever seen anyone send himself off.

Meanwhile, scenes on the pitch were chaotic. Players were pushing and shoving each other, as spectators clambered over the fence to join in. I was happy to stand and watch – I didn't fancy getting punched again. Roy was less content to take a passive role and was screaming abuse in the general direction of the Folkestone players, while officials from both sides were trying to calm things down.

When the dust had settled, we were treated to the satisfying sight of Cugley being sent off despite only just recovering consciousness. But an even greater moment came deep into the eight minutes of injury time when Junior Crooks got a late winner and we had finally beaten Folkestone. That was when I discovered something about winning. When you beat a team you really hate, it feels so much better than a standard win against someone like Corinthian Casuals.

A sizeable police contingent had gathered and the players were escorted off the pitch. It was later reported that, when Keith Bradbrook took his socks off after the game, he had abrasions from knee to ankle on both legs – and he was wearing shin pads. Emblem could barely walk and Broadway's face was badly bruised.

I had never experienced such joy after a game of football. Beating Folkestone was everything I'd wanted in life. It didn't matter that I got home after midnight. This was redemption.

Despite not being able to afford it, I couldn't resist going to Hayes Lane a few days later for the league game against Harrow Borough. If we won, we'd go top of the Isthmian League

(Division 1). And Bromley carried on where they left off, easing to a comfortable 3-1 lead which they never looked like losing.

It was all quite an undramatic and peaceful affair after Wednesday. Or at least it was until Junior Crooks decided to headbutt the aptly named Fowles, after a tussle near the corner flag. That was the cue for further mayhem, with Crooks and Fowles swapping punches, before Fowles' teammates went to his aid and chased Crooks around the pitch. While this was going on, Harrow's Thomas connected with a wild swing at Derek Brown, while other players were content with the usual pushing and shoving.

On Wednesday it had been Duffy running towards the dressing room after knocking someone out cold. Today it was Crooks running towards safety, hotly pursued by most of the Harrow players. I felt that Bromley's discipline was slipping.

In the end, Crooks, Fowles and Thomas were sent off, which meant that in two games I had seen the sending off of two Bromley players, two Folkestone players and two Harrow players. I'd seen a full-scale riot, both home and away. And in the process, I'd seen Bromley get through to the second qualifying round of the FA Trophy and go top of the league.

Anything after that was going to be an anticlimax, and so it proved when Woking knocked us out of the Trophy in the next round. The week got even worse three days later, when England failed to qualify for the World Cup in Argentina by only beating Italy 2-0. They needed to win by at least five, but even the addition of wingers Steve Coppell and Peter Barnes, plus free-scoring Everton striker Bob Latchford, wasn't enough and, barring a miracle that would involve Italy failing to beat useless Luxembourg at home, England were out.

There was further disappointment to come when Bromley

just missed out on promotion, finishing third by the narrowest of margins.

But although none of this could dim the satisfaction of beating Folkestone, I was sick of watching them play Bromley. So when the FA Cup draw the following season brought the teams together for the sixth time in three seasons, I couldn't bring myself to go. It was just as well – we lost 2-1, with Junior Crooks getting the goal.

Not long after that came an event that I wouldn't have missed for anything in the world. It was something I had waited for my whole life. I finally got to see Bromley compete for a major trophy at Wembley.

CHAPTER NINE

On a cold, late-November night in 1979, I once again found myself battling through heavy rain and gale-force winds to watch Bromley. But this time, I was making my way down Olympic Way from Wembley Park Tube station.

As I struggled against the elements, I kept focused on the twin towers ahead, filled with excitement. Wembley Stadium. This was where Bromley had won the FA Amateur Cup. And where England had won the World Cup.

When I got there, I just stood and stared, thinking of Eric Fright in 1949 and Bobby Moore in 1966, lifting the most important trophies of their lifetimes. I was getting soaked through, but it didn't seem to matter.

After a few minutes, I reluctantly dragged myself away, turned right and immediately caught sight of my destination, Wembley Arena. I had a ticket for the Berger Isthmian League Five-a-Side Championship, a brand-new trophy that was the brainwave of the league's visionary chairman, Barry East. In true visionary style, he had set his sights high and named it the Prince Philip Cup.

Although the venue wasn't quite the same as Wembley Stadium in terms of size or anything else, it was still pretty impressive, having recently hosted the *Evening Standard* five-a-side competition. This meant that Bromley would soon be treading the same cloth-covered boards and passing off the same advert-decked walls as some of the all-time football greats had done on the BBC's *Sportsnight*.

I found my seat with the help of a uniformed steward and silently congratulated myself on splashing out £3.80 on one of the more expensive tickets. I was sitting quite high up behind one of the goals but the view was really good – it reminded me of being in the upper stalls at the Bromley Odeon.

Bromley didn't have a realistic chance of winning the tournament – they played in Division 1 of the Isthmian League, whereas everyone else played in the Premier League – but I was still looking forward to seeing some of the giants of the non-league game, even though they had stomped all over my prepubescent football dreams. The likes of Enfield, Hendon and Wycombe Wanderers.

As I ran through the team lists in the programme, I kept coming across names that struck fear into the hearts of those of us with an encyclopaedic knowledge of the Berger (formerly Rothmans) Isthmian League.

There was Hendon legend Rod Haider, who had scored against Newcastle in the FA Cup; Enfield's free-scoring Ronnie Howell; and Walthamstow Avenue's goal machine Bobby Tapin, who really did score a tap-in the only time I'd seen him play.

This only added to the anxiety I felt in knowing that I wouldn't have the luxury of slowly easing into the tournament by watching other teams. Bromley were on first.

Their opponents in the opening round were Slough Town, a team who lived up to their nickname of 'The Rebels' by running onto the pitch wilfully wearing all red, when the programme said they'd be playing in their traditional yellow shirts with blue shorts.

I nervously demolished a Mars Bar as their players warmed up. As I was putting the wrapper in my pocket, I noticed that the bar had been made in Slough. Was this some kind of sign? I was pretty sure it was, although I had no idea what it meant.

My ambition for the tournament was for Bromley to cause an upset against Slough, who were, after all, adrift at the bottom of the Isthmian Premier League. If that was a step too far for my team, a goal would do. That should be achievable, especially with the great Butch Dunn named as a starter.

I had to reassess that target as soon as Bromley followed Slough out through the white gate in the wall surrounding the pitch. My heart sank when I saw that the bearded figure of Butch Dunn was missing, and in his place was the far less prolific Sid Williamson. I decided that, as long as the team weren't humiliated, I'd be happy.

The point was that I'd be able to tell my grandchildren that I'd seen Bromley play at Wembley, even though Wembley would have an asterisk after it. What I probably wouldn't mention was that I went there on my own, unable to persuade even Roy to come with me.

The game started in typical Bromley fashion when they went a goal down after two minutes. Goalkeeper Malcolm Broadway probably should have done better, but ever since I'd seen him get kicked in the face, I found it hard to criticise him. A couple of minutes later though, all was forgotten. I leaped into the air as the magnificent Sid Williamson, whom I had never doubted, scored a superb individual goal to make it 1-1.

After top scorer Ian Parsons put Bromley ahead just after half-time, I began squirming around in my seat, looking at my watch and staring beseechingly at the official timekeeper, Reg Paine, who was sitting pitchside. The seconds ticked by agonisingly slowly, and I was convinced Slough's equaliser was only a matter of time.

This went on for four of the longest minutes in the history of football, while Broadway kept his side in the game with some brilliant saves. I was sitting behind the Bromley goal and, each time Slough attacked, I could see our keeper positioning himself to deal with the threat.

I must have glanced over at Reg Paine at least another dozen times, wondering if his clock had stopped or if a Far Eastern betting syndicate had got to him. But just as I was about to give up on the match ever ending, referee Ernie Day signalled full-time.

As the whistle echoed around the vast arena, I felt a lot more excited than the Bromley players, whose outward displays of emotion were limited to the odd smile or handshake. I knew I was getting carried away, imagining the Bromley players passing the cup around after leaving a trail of slain giants in their wake, but that didn't stop me relishing the moment. We'd made it! The quarter-final of the Prince Philip Cup. The last eight of the ultimate test of five-a-side non-league football. I thought my heart rate would slow down after the drama of hanging on to the slenderest of leads but, if anything, it rose as the full significance of the next game sank in.

Barking were up against Billericay. And Bromley would be playing the winner.

I wanted Billericay to win, mainly because they weren't Barking. This was why I found myself shouting 'Come on, Billericay' when it went to a penalty shootout. But my motivational efforts failed to inspire them. Barking converted their fifth penalty and Billericay didn't.

Barking. The one team we could never beat. Ever.

Barking. Who had just got through to the second round of the FA Cup on the previous Saturday.

Barking. Who had beaten Bromley 8-0 and 7-0 in consecutive seasons.

Barking. The reigning Isthmian League champions.

I wandered around the arena in an attempt to walk off some of the stress. Wembley was about three-quarters full, which meant the crowd wasn't threatening the attendance record set by a David Cassidy concert in 1971, and the fans were a little more muted than they would have been for the puppy-eyed heart-throb. Non-league fans tend to internalise their appreciation more than hysterical, hormonal teenagers.

By the time I got back to my seat, I was feeling a lot more relaxed. I'd come to terms with my team's inevitable fate. I then sat back and watched Enfield and Wycombe swat aside their opposition to join us in the quarter-finals, glad that we wouldn't have to play them further along in the competition. Being alongside teams like these was a measure of how well Bromley had done to make it this far.

Our quarter-final was first up, and by the time referee Geoff Privett blew his whistle to get the game underway, I had again taken comfort in the fact that we were technically one of the top eight five-a-side teams in the Isthmian League, and that losing to Barking would be no disgrace.

This calm, philosophical acceptance lasted precisely forty-five seconds. That was when Derek Brown, Bromley's curly haired version of Kevin Keegan, scored with a lovely shot across the face of the goal to give us a shock lead. Suddenly, I found myself overwhelmed by a succession of irrational thoughts. What if we actually won this game? What if we got through to the semi-finals, where we'd be one of the top four five-a-side teams in the Isthmian League? What if Barking didn't score the two last-minute goals I was expecting?

And in the end, they didn't score those two last-minute goals. They scored one, seconds before the final whistle, to draw level. It doesn't matter, I told myself. It's only a five-a-side game.

That piece of psychology didn't work as well as I'd hoped. When Barking drew level, I was crushed. The familiar feeling of disappointment replaced the novelty of hope. We had come so close. But now it was going to penalties. And in my experience, we converted fewer penalties than pretty much everyone else in Berger/Rothmans Isthmian League history.

As Ian Parsons took the first kick – and comfortably scored – my chest was thudding so fast, I was convinced I was about to have a heart attack. I looked around and was relieved to see a man in his forties and a woman around my age in St John Ambulance uniforms. I quite fancied the woman, but refrained from asking her out, as there was a strong possibility that our life together could be cut tragically short if things got any more tense.

I peeked through my fingers as the Barking number four took a stuttering run-up, hit the ball cleanly – and Broadway dived the right way and saved magnificently.

Bromley were through into uncharted territory and my poise disappeared as I leaped up and down, shouting 'Yes!' repeatedly.

My next instinct was to rush to the phone box I'd noticed on the way in, to spread the exciting news, but I couldn't think of anyone who'd be remotely interested. I sat down, but was so restless that I got up again and began to jog on the spot. I wasn't sure why, although it might well have been some kind of nervous reaction.

By now, I was totally absorbed in the Prince Philip Cup, its position in the football trophy hierarchy having improved as the evening went on. Although the next match would decide our opponents in the semi-final, it was barely worth watching.

It was obvious that Enfield were going to beat Walthamstow Avenue and, naturally, they obliged.

The final two quarter-finals passed by in a blur. I was becoming increasingly nervous. My breathing got increasingly shallow as I waited for THE semi-final. I studied the programme in detail in an attempt to distract myself. I must have read the 'Welcome to you all' message from the honorary secretary of the Berger Isthmian League at least five times. And as he thanked Colonel Satterthwaite, Miss Pippa Ryde and the Berger Paint Company, I tried not to think about what lay ahead.

But that proved impossible. Enfield cast a giant shadow. There was no escaping them.

They were an Isthmian League superpower, whose trophy cabinet would have required constant reinforcement. They'd even won the Anglo-Italian Amateur Cup, which also made them an Anglo-Italian superpower.

Even more impressively, four of the five players who'd be facing Bromley in just a few minutes had just been picked to represent the Isthmian League in the Office Cleaning Services Inter-League Cup, a competition so obscure that even I had never heard of it.

All Bromley had won in the decade I'd been watching them was that (admittedly gigantic) Kent Senior Cup and the Bromley Hospital Cup, which appeared to be open only to Bromley and a couple of hopeless lower-league teams whose home ground was in the general vicinity of Bromley Hospital.

Yet here we were, meeting Enfield in the final four of a major (-ish) competition. My mouth was dry and I felt light-headed.

It was rumoured that Wales's blood-red rugby shirts were designed in order to inspire intimidation. Enfield's white shirts with blue collars had the same effect on me. Enfield. The team that had ruined my childhood were warming up right in front of my eyes.

All four of their outfield players looked in a different class. Every cleanly hit shot ripped past their keeper and caressed the net with a whooshing sound. No wonder Moore, Gibson, Jennings and O'Sullivan had been picked to play in the Office Cleaning Services Inter-League Cup.

My hands were sweating so much, they'd stuck to the programme I was clutching, leaving a large palm print over the Berger advert on the back. Yet the first half was much closer than it had any right to be, and Eddie Read might even have put Bromley ahead, had he not stumbled when clean through.

My legs were twitching wildly and I could barely bring myself to watch by the time the interval arrived and we were still level. Were Enfield toying with us? The other option, that Bromley might be playing quite well, never occurred to me.

It was at this point that I realised the major flaw in five-a-side football. With a half-time break of only a minute, there was no time to reflect on the first half over a cup of tea, a cigarette and, in an ideal world, a slice of Battenberg cake. This only added to the agony I was enduring.

And it got even worse in the second half. With time running out, Ian Parsons tried a shot from around twenty yards out and his effort rebounded off Enfield keeper Steve Terry's thigh, onto the inside of the post, then back into his grateful arms. That was when I realised it was his day and that, if the game went to penalties, we were doomed.

The game went to penalties. And that was when the stress finally got to me. As Sid Williamson ran up to take Bromley's first kick, Terry seemed to grow in size. He looked huge, as did his gloves, and the goal began to shrink right in front of my eyes. Was this really happening? Or was this some kind of anxiety-induced hallucination?

Somehow, Williamson's effort squeezed into the mini-goal past the giant goalkeeper and Bromley led. Now it was Enfield's turn and, this time, the goal seemed to grow while Malcolm Broadway shrank. It came as no surprise when Tony Jennings, Enfield legend that he was, scored with ease.

Bromley, surprisingly, made it two from two thanks to Derek Brown.

AND THEN JOHN TONE, ENFIELD'S SUBSTITUTE, MISSED.

All I remember is gulping for air and rubbing my eyes to check that they weren't deceiving me. Bromley beating Enfield was one of those things that simply didn't happen in real life, like an oversized Great Dane winning the Grand National, or an Englishman winning Wimbledon.

But the announcer confirmed it. Bromley were in the final of a major tournament. I just sat there in shock, gaping like a goldfish as the other semi-final followed the form book and Wycombe thrashed Dagenham 5-2.

Wycombe were another team who had ruined my child-hood. The first Bromley game I ever saw was against them, and it lulled me into a false impression of what life held in store for a Bromley fan. We won 3-2. I mistakenly thought every game would be like that. They weren't. A season later we kicked off against the same opponents. That time we lost 5-0.

And now, ten years later, we were playing them again. I could feel my sweat turn cold as my round-collared shirt clung to me. My head was swimming and several times I wondered if I was in a dream.

I pinched myself hard. It really hurt. I wasn't dreaming. Bromley really had made the final. It was a thought that made me feel faint again and I tucked into yet another Mars Bar. I just wanted the game to start.

And then the teams ran out – and this was the moment I

knew for certain that I was a victim of a stress-induced hallucination.

Bobby Moore came out first, followed by Geoff Hurst,
Jimmy Greaves and Arsenal's Frank McLintock. Finally, Jess
Conrad from the Sex Pistols' film *The Great Rock 'n' Roll Swin-
dle* took his place in goal, wearing a black tracksuit. At least it
wasn't a bin liner.

Had Wycombe signed them all since the semi-final? Not
only was it unfair, it was also highly unlikely.

Then it got even weirder, as a bunch of England cricketers
wearing football kit, including Mickey Stewart, Graham
Roope and Geoff Arnold, strolled out at a more sedate pace. It
was only when the announcer, who sounded suspiciously like
Jimmy Hill, said that this was a celebrity charity game before
the final that I realised I wasn't seeing things.

Moore's team were called 'The Goaldiggers'. I felt this was
an excellent name and it was a shame the same thought hadn't
been given to the opposition's name, who went under the less
flamboyant banner of 'Doug Insole's Team of Test Cricketers'.

Normally, I would have relished the chance to watch some
of my favourite sportsmen play for a good cause, but charity
could wait.

Bromley's biggest game since 1949 was coming up next.

Once Moore and Co. had thankfully departed the arena, it
was time. Watching Bromley jog out for a cup final was almost
too much for my nerves to bear. I was sure I was going to faint.
The lights felt bright and hot, and I was rigid with tension.

When Wycombe went close with an early effort, my heart
felt as though it was about to burst through my chest and I sur-
reptitiously edged nearer the St John Ambulance duo.

It was the most exciting game I had ever seen. Wycombe
went ahead; Bromley equalised. Wycombe regained the lead,

but Bromley, in stark contrast to the pre-Biddle Bromley, refused to give up and soon made it 2-2.

The relief brought by the full-time whistle was short-lived. The announcer said that there would now be extra time, consisting of two halves of two minutes each. And then penalties. I seriously doubted if my nervous system could withstand the strain of another shootout, let alone one in a final. I had only recently found out what an unenjoyable, agonising experience it could be supporting a successful team.

As extra time got underway, the neutrals had all adopted Bromley, the underdogs. Every attack was greeted with the loudest cheers I'd ever heard for my team.

Suddenly, a Wycombe attack was broken up by Eddie Read, who found Ian Parsons in space. Parsons calmly swept the ball under the diving Chris Way and it was 3-2 to Bromley. I couldn't watch any more. There were just thirty seconds standing between Bromley and a proper silver trophy won at Wembley.

I shut my eyes and counted down: 'One Mississippi, two Mississippi, three Mississippi...' As I did this, I was acutely aware of every groan, every shout, every 'Come on Bromley!'

I'd reached 'twenty-seven Mississippi' when I heard the final whistle. I opened my eyes and the Bromley players were leaping around in celebration, joined by supporters, old and new. I was too stunned to join them. Besides, what if the officials decided that we'd fielded an ineligible player and kicked us out? Or what if timekeeper Reg Paine suddenly realised that he'd made a mistake and called the teams back to play an extra minute, which would be enough time for Wycombe to equalise? And what if a mysterious Far Eastern betting syndicate was found to have had a hand in the result, as was strongly rumoured to have happened in the *Evening Standard* five-a-side competition?

But as the presentations got underway, it finally sunk in. Bromley had won the Prince Philip Cup. And to make life even better, Ian Parsons received his Player of the Night silver salver from the *Evening Standard*.

That was when I did something that was easily the most embarrassing thing I'd ever done at a football match.

It was worse than asking an assistant groundsman for his autograph after mistaking him for a player. Worse than trying to clamber over the picket fence at Hayes Lane, getting my foot stuck and falling flat on my face. It was even more humiliating than loudly starting a 'Give me a B, Give me an R' chant at Maidstone and no one joining in.

I burst into tears. In front of 3,000 people.

These were tears of pride. No one, including me, had given Bromley a chance. But they'd gone out there and beaten some of the biggest names in the non-league universe.

I just wished Caroline, a nurse I'd been going out with for a couple of weeks, had been there with me to see history being made, but she'd said she was working nights.

I then drifted back to the time when I was fourteen and a couple of skinheads wearing Chelsea scarves had approached me in Warren Avenue Park and asked me who I supported. When I defiantly said 'Bromley', they burst out laughing.

Well, they wouldn't be laughing now.

Usually, I like to leave a game as soon as the whistle goes, but not this time. Half an hour later, I was the only one in the entire Wembley Arena still sitting down. I was still soaking it all up, reliving the goals and saves while they were fresh in my mind. I didn't want to leave.

It was almost as though I sensed that it would be the last time I'd see Bromley play for thirty-two years.

Part Two

CHAPTER TEN

I moved around a lot in the next thirty-two years. I was living in Leeds when my girlfriend became my wife, and Manchester when Bromley finally got promoted. I was in New Zealand when Bobby Moore played at Hayes Lane, and the USA when the chairman's brother-in-law, despite having no relevant experience, was made the club's manager.

Although geographical reasons (combined with being permanently broke) stopped me from watching Bromley in person, I kept in touch, wherever I was in the world. This was thanks to my mum sending me the *Bromley & Kentish Times* and The Grubby sending me the occasional *News Shopper*, south-east London and north-west Kent's invaluable local rag.

On the warm, late-August day when Bromley drew 1-1 at home to Slough (Butch Dunn scoring his fifth goal in as many games), thus preserving their unbeaten record in the league, I was getting married to Caroline, the nurse I'd met in Leeds, at a small church in rural Devon. Unlike Derek (aka Del the Biker) on his wedding day, I resisted the urge to dash along to Hayes Lane after the ceremony to catch the second half. Besides, I would never have got there in time.

We'd moved to Manchester by the time Bromley returned

to the Isthmian League (Premier Division) thanks to a Junior Crooks goal sealing a vital win against Finchley. I tried to picture it in my mind, but that was unsatisfactory, since I didn't have much to work on – the description in the paper of 'a tidy finish from close range' was sparse.

I also missed out on seeing Bromley play Chertsey Town in the preliminary round of the FA Cup the following season, my excuse being that we now lived in New Zealand. I'd been offered a job in Wellington, and both Caroline and I liked the idea of a fresh start.

Despite the distance, I still worried about my team's prospects since goals had been hard to come by in the early games of the campaign and Chertsey had made a decent start in the Athenian League.

A week later, my anxiety turned to joyous disbelief as I opened the blue airmail envelope from my mum, unfolded the back page of the *Bromley & Kentish Times* and saw that Bromley had managed to win by a record score, 12-1. I read, and re-read, descriptions of each goal, including all four of Galloway's and each of Tomlin's hat-trick.

Another thing I wished I'd witnessed was seeing Simon Keith in a Bromley shirt. Keith had fled his native Canada for England after life under the spotlight became too much and ended up in Bromley, where no one, including players, officials and supporters (like me), knew anything about him.

His story – when it emerged – made headline news in several national papers. Because when he was twenty and seriously ill, Simon Keith had undergone a heart-transplant operation. Wanting to ease his way back into football, and since he had relatives living nearby, he joined Bromley. After proving himself as far too good for the Isthmian League (even the Premier Division), he confessed to club director John Fiornini that he had played for Millwall before undergoing the operation.

Dave Roberts

I also missed out on the great acorn assault at St Albans, when Bromley goalkeeper Nicky Sullivan was pelted with acorns by unruly home fans, in a story that once again made the national press. It was described in poetic tones by the *Guardian* as 'Trouble at normally sleepy, leafy Clarence Park'. Was this belated payback for when Bromley fans had lobbed acorns at St Albans keeper Howard a decade and a half previously? Should I write to the *Guardian* and tell them the full story? Considering I was now on the other side of the world and hadn't thrown a single acorn myself, I felt I was probably safe from prosecution.

Nature also played a big part in Bromley's next appearance in the headlines, when the ground fell victim to Britain's first hurricane in three hundred years. Despite reassurances from the BBC weatherman Michael Fish that the hurricane wouldn't happen, it did.

An entire section of the Hayes Lane roof was blown away, turnstiles were ripped from their moorings and fences were flung down. The pitch was covered in broken tiles and surrounding roads blocked by fallen trees. (In Sevenoaks, where I'd gone to school, six of the seven oak trees that had given the town its name were blown down and I wondered if it would have to change its name to Oneoak.)

The next day, over seven hundred spectators turned up to see Bromley beat Kingstonian 2-0. And the following year, I missed out on a once-in-a-lifetime chance to see Bobby Moore play at Hayes Lane, by which time there was no trace of the damage done to the ground.

It was a match arranged to help Paul Buckland, a young man who had lost his leg following an injury in a Sunday League game, and a team of England stars were up against an Old Bromley XI. Lining up for the internationals alongside household names like Moore, Mike Summerbee, Alan Mullery

113

and John Hollins was the lesser-known Mike O'Connor, who played for the Old Bromleians seventh team. By coincidence, this was the same side that the manager, Bob 'The Cat' Bevan, played for in goal.

And Bobby Moore wasn't the only World Cup winner to play at Hayes Lane in the 1980s. Ossie Ardiles was in the Spurs reserves side that played Charlton Athletic in a Football Combination game, when he was on his way back from injury. Moore and Ardiles had more in common than playing on the Hayes Lane turf. They had both sung on number one singles and had both experienced winning at Wembley.

But the biggest, most exciting news of the decade from Hayes Lane (via the *News Shopper*) was the announcement that Bromley would be signing England international Kenny Sansom. He'd been capped around eighty times during his time with Arsenal and Crystal Palace and would now be playing for Bromley. Terms had been agreed with the thirty-four-year-old left back and he was due to sign by the end of the week. I couldn't wait for the next *News Shopper* to arrive, so I could read about his debut in a Bromley shirt. The prospect was enough to affect my sleep all week.

When the paper finally arrived, I eagerly turned to the back page. There was no mention of our glorious new signing anywhere. It was only when I came to a small paragraph inside, saying that Sansom hadn't turned up, that I realised, once again, that my dreams had been crushed.

The nearest Bromley came to the twin towers in the 1980s was a relatively glorious FA Cup run right at the end of the decade. I would have loved to have seen the four goals in four games from fan favourite Jerry Dolke, an all-action centre forward, which took Bromley to the brink of the first round proper.

But Wembley continued to be a (very) distant dream,

although I promised myself that I would come back from wherever I was if Bromley ever played there. This did not include Wembley Arena.

The following decade was bookended by two relegations to the Isthmian League (Division 1) but, in between, there were many occasions I wished I could have witnessed.

The first time I felt the pangs of missing Hayes Lane in the new decade came when St Albans visited for a league game. Included in their line-up was goalkeeper Paul 'Mad Dog' O'Reilly, who was also a DJ on Chiltern Radio (he'd been given his nickname by fellow Chiltern DJ Paul 'The Hypnotist' McKenna). 'Mad Dog' O'Reilly playing in the Diadora Isthmian League, as it was now called, was the most exciting pop music/football crossover since I'd found out about Knotty's famous cousins.

O'Reilly also played cricket and had his own painting and decorating business, but I found that less fascinating.

An even more famous name to appear at Hayes Lane during the 1990s was the Olympic gold medallist Daley Thompson who, for reasons which were never explained, turned out for Wimbledon in a preseason friendly. Proof that he really should have stuck to the decathlon came when his own goal levelled the scores just before half-time.

Also in the Wimbledon line-up that day, adding weight to the theory that they weren't taking the match entirely seriously, was Wolf, the arch-villain from the TV series *Gladiators*.

I would have loved to have been at Hayes Lane a few seasons later to see Jon Goodman, one of new manager George Wakeling's first signings, who was sold for a record £34,500 despite the fact that most Bromley fans had never seen him play. He'd only taken part in a handful of preseason friendlies when Millwall put in the offer, which was gratefully accepted. Goodman went on to play in the Premier League for Wimbledon (a significant upgrade on Daley Thompson and Wolf from *Gladiators*) and won four caps with the Republic of Ireland.

There was sadness, too, when the *Bromley & Kentish Times* brought news of the death of Miss Peters at the age of ninety-two. She was the last of the Peters sisters and the last surviving supporter to have watched the 1911 FA Amateur Cup final. Although unable to get to Hayes Lane in later years, she regularly phoned John Self, by now a committee member, for the latest result and a brief match report.

I had always been too intimidated to actually talk to this Peters sister (or indeed any of the others), but still felt huge fondness for her. She was Bromley royalty and I hoped they kept her seat at the front of the supporters' club coach empty as a tribute.

But the biggest news arrived one morning in October 1992. I tore open a large, brown envelope addressed with The Grubby's scrawled handwriting, eager for news of Bromley's game at Harrow Borough and the name of our opponents in the FA Trophy third round qualifying draw. But nothing could have prepared me for the story splashed across the front page of the *News Shopper*, which was inside the envelope.

A fire had devastated Hayes Lane, burning down the stand before spreading to the rest of the ground. Twenty-five firemen had fought for over two hours to contain the blaze. Despite the positive noises from defiant chairman Glyn Beverly, it seemed that this could be the end for Bromley Football Club. The ground would be closed for several months at best, which would mean no income for the rest of the year. And that was the best possible scenario.

A poignant photo of committee member Brian Traer, looking forlorn in the charred remains of the gutted stand, surrounded by debris, brought home the extent of the damage.

The report ended with news that some memorabilia had also

116

been destroyed. My heart sank even further as I realised this probably included the photo on the wall of the tea hut, in glorious black and white, showing Eric Fright being held aloft by his Bromley teammates whilst proudly clutching the FA Amateur Cup, the picture that had fired my imagination and inspired my Wembley dreams.

The only bright spot came with the news that at least a couple of parts of the ground had survived, although this reprieve proved to be short-lived. A few weeks later, a stray firework from nearby Norman Park was blamed for a second fire at Hayes Lane, doing further extensive damage. It took the best part of a year to get back to normal, but eventually the ground reopened and Bromley had survived the worst threat to their existence in the club's history.

Once Hayes Lane was restored to its former glory, I would have dearly loved to have been there for one of the most satisfying wins since I'd been away. It came against Chesham United in the third qualifying round of the FA Cup. Chesham were unimpressed by having to visit Hayes Lane. In their programme the week before the game, they complained that in various cup competitions recently they 'hadn't exactly drawn the glamorous sides', before putting the boot in by adding 'In the FA Cup we are away to Bromley.'

Much to my satisfaction, we beat them 2-1, with goals from Woolf (not the Gladiator) and Rawlings. But what made this even more satisfying was that the goals were scored against a man who had won the European Cup when he was with Liverpool, Bruce Grobbelaar.

Even though he must have been close to pensioner status by the time he ended up at Chesham, he was still the most famous goalkeeper ever to have played against Bromley. According to The Grubby (whom I'd once started calling The Grubbelaar since he fancied himself as a goalkeeper), both goals were high quality and would have beaten Grobbelaar in his prime.

One Bromley player from that era that I particularly wish I could have seen must sadly remain nameless. He was hugely talented by all accounts, with an eye for goal. But a clue to the slight flaws in his personality can be found in his player profile, where he listed his hobbies as 'smoking and drinking'.

Proof of the former came in a preseason game, when he was taken off during the second half. Instead of going back to the dugout, he hurdled the fence, approached a small group of Bromley fans and said, 'Any of you £@$%$s got a Woodbine?'

As for the latter, on the Friday night before a big game he was (allegedly) seen staggering around Trafalgar Square at 3 a.m. looking for a night bus, shirt unbuttoned, eating a hot dog. Twelve hours later he was lining up for Bromley and scoring a memorable goal.

He sounded like my kind of footballer.

The next update from The Grubby brought unwelcome news regarding a tree I had grown oddly fond of – the large oak on the terrace at normally sleepy St Albans. The club had had it removed. I thought this may have been at the request of a long line of visiting goalkeepers, fed up with acorn attacks, but apparently the tree had fallen victim to some kind of disease and was chopped down not long before the new millennium.

(Continuing the St Albans theme, the *Wellington Evening Post* – our local paper – carried a small piece about an English medium-pace bowler who had taken all ten wickets in an innings for Hertfordshire against Staffordshire in a Minor Counties cricket match. His name? Paul 'Mad Dog' O'Reilly, who, ten years earlier, had helped St Albans to a 1-1 draw at Hayes Lane.)

But the last piece of news I got from home at the end of the century was also one of the saddest. The passing of another of Bromley's royalty – our greatest-ever player.

In the season when we won the first-ever Amateur Cup final to be played at Wembley, George Brown scored a hundred goals, after getting ninety-nine the previous season. He went on to captain England and was clearly one of the best amateurs in the history of the game. One thing I could never understand was why one of the bigger clubs hadn't signed him. He could have become one of the greats.

I only found out the reason a couple of years after he died. Amongst his possessions were a bundle of letters from the country's biggest clubs, such as Arsenal, Newcastle United, Charlton Athletic and Liverpool, asking him to play for them. He politely wrote back to each club, thanking them for their interest, but insisting he was a family man, happy with his life as it was and that playing for Bromley on Saturday afternoons was all he wanted.

He stayed with Bromley for twenty years, and tried to retire several times, but committee members always managed to talk him out of it.

Several years later, Roy the dustman, when he wasn't selling Golden Goal tickets at Hayes Lane, was hard at work on his usual round. He was working hard because his crew had been tipped off that the council had sent a time-and-motion team to make sure that they were operating as efficiently as possible. Roy must have thought he was seeing things when he peered through the thick lenses in his glasses and saw a familiar face amongst the men with clipboards and stopwatches. It was George Brown, and he and Roy spent their allotted time together talking not about the speed of rubbish disposal but about their shared passion, Bromley FC.

And it was rubbish that became a recurring theme in the early years of the new millennium. Some of the worst games ever seen by Bromley fans took place during this period. It was so depressing that match reports got too hard to read and I just skipped through them.

One of the few bright spots came when Bromley won the London Senior Cup in 2003, beating Ford United 1-0. To celebrate, a video was released of the game. Well, 99 per cent of the game. In typical Bromley fashion, whoever had filmed it managed to miss the only goal.

But things began to improve when Jerry Dolke, scorer of those goals during the FA Cup run, took over the club and made his brother-in-law, Mark Goldberg, the manager. This was a surprise since his managerial experience was limited to being player-manager of Kent League side Beckenham Town and 'running Bromley Under-9s for a couple of seasons'. He was perhaps better known for losing every penny of his £23 million fortune having bought Crystal Palace but somehow with the Selhurst Road ground not included in the deal.

But it worked better than anyone expected and, in 2006, Goldberg, who had developed a habit of storming out of the club and rejoining not long after, took Bromley to the highest level in their history, the Blue Square Conference South. We were now playing in the sixth tier of the football pyramid.

Since I'd been away from Hayes Lane, I had got married, had three children, gone through a phase of wearing dungarees (influenced by Dexy's Midnight Runners) and bought a house in a leafy Wellington suburb.

I'd then got divorced, worn a 'Frankie says Relax' T-shirt, lost my job and house through long-term illness and gone from twelve to twenty-five stone.

After that, I'd got remarried, started wearing a fishing hat (influenced by the Stone Roses), gone from twenty-five to twelve stone and moved to the US, to live with my new wife Liz's parents in Hartford, Connecticut.

And it was there, at the age of fifty-six, that I saw Bromley on TV for the first time in my life, losing to Leyton Orient in the first round of the FA Cup. It looked close (not that you can tell much in one minute twenty-six seconds of highlights) and Orient's George Porter, who scored a wonder goal and then got Aaron Rhule sent off, was the difference between the sides.

But I wasn't that disappointed. It was a measure of Bromley's progress that they were on the highlights programme. If anything, I felt a mix of pride and sadness – pride at getting that far and being on the telly, and sadness that being flat broke made it unlikely I'd get to see the new-look Bromley for a while.

But then I had an incredible piece of luck. One that meant I wouldn't have to follow the crucial FA Trophy third qualifying round game against Didcot Town on Twitter a fortnight later, as I'd originally planned.

Instead, I'd be at Hayes Lane to watch it in person.

CHAPTER ELEVEN

There were two impossible-to-ignore signs that 2011/12 was going to be the season Bromley finally returned to Wembley.

The first came completely out of the blue – I got a phone call from my publisher at Random House, announcing that one of my books, *32 Programmes*, had been shortlisted for the William Hill Sports Book of the Year award and that they would be flying me from the US to London for the ceremony.

Breathless with excitement, I got off the phone and went online. And there it was in black and white – the day after landing in the UK the Bromley v Didcot Town FA Trophy game would be taking place.

The second impossible-to-ignore sign came when I then rushed to the website of the *Witney Gazette*, which covered Didcot Town news, and discovered that their new signing, ex-£1.5 million Newcastle striker Paul Robinson, who was once preferred up front to Alan Shearer, was cup-tied and wouldn't be playing. In his place would be a sixteen-year-old kid called Uche Ikpeazu.

When I checked on the Bromley forum (which had taken the place of week-old copies of the *Bromley & Kentish Times* as my go-to source of Bromley news), I saw that the fans seemed unconcerned. Their main focus was trying to guess what Didcot's nickname was – theories put forward included Diddymen, Diddlers, Diddycoys and, implausibly, Didcot Diddy Diddlers.

By the time we landed at Heathrow, I was more convinced than ever that this was going to be Bromley's year. The reason for the sky-high optimism was that a third impossible-to-ignore sign had emerged while we were stuck in a holding pattern above London waiting to land – and I was given a clear view through the airplane window of Wembley Stadium.

It was a shame that I'd only be able to go to one game on Bromley's road there, but I'd always promised myself that, if we did make the final, I would fly back for it. I'd have to make do with following the rest of the run on Twitter.

The next morning, on the way to the Didcot game, and trying to ignore the jet lag, I went to visit my dad, who had just turned ninety-one. He was in a nursing home in Clapham and, when I arrived at reception, the nurse told me not to expect too much, as he'd been having a few problems recently, and had been getting a bit confused. In a recent phone call, I wasn't sure he'd registered the bit about my coming over for the awards, but that didn't matter – I was just happy to see him and he seemed glad to see me. We spent an hour together before I could see he was getting tired and wanted a nap. I told him I was going to watch Bromley and he nodded, with a trace of a smile.

Before I could go to Hayes Lane, I had to meet a man for lunch. His name was T. J. Herbert and he'd rung me one morning to say that he was a film producer and was interested in turning another of my books, *The Bromley Boys*, into a film. He was clearly deluded, since hardly anyone had ever shown any interest in reading it, let alone making a film of it.

Still, it meant a free prematch lunch, so I was happy to go along with it. T. J., a handsome man in his mid-thirties, was what could best be described as a colourful dresser, combining red cord trousers with a yellow jacket and a straw hat. It turned out that he hadn't actually produced a film before, although as an actor he had once played Klaus, a Swedish hitchhiker who had very briefly appeared in *EastEnders* (a programme my wife Liz and I avidly followed back home in Connecticut).

T. J. had a highly ambitious shortlist of actors and directors for *The Bromley Boys*. By the time I was finishing off my apple strudel, I realised that this was a film that would never get made.

Despite that, there was a bit of a spring in my step as I took the familiar walk to Hayes Lane half an hour later. It had been an entertaining lunch and I'd loved seeing my dad beforehand. The visit had reminded me how much I missed him.

Eventually my thoughts turned to football, but when I found myself idly thinking about beating that 12-1 scoreline at Chertsey Town, I had to stop myself. That kind of thinking can be dangerous.

Instead, as I passed the horses grazing in the paddock outside the entrance to the ground, I thought about another incident I'd missed through living abroad – the sight of one of Charlie King's committee members running across the grass at high speed, with the ball he'd been despatched to collect tucked under his arm. The reason for this urgency was that he was being pursued by a bull.

For me, the paddock was as much a part of the Hayes Lane experience as the bowls club on the opposite side of the drive. It was comforting to know that, however much the club changed, these would always be there.

When I got through the turnstiles, I decided to sit in the new stand for the first time. This was to avoid another potential jinx – my only other visit to Hayes Lane in the past thirty-two years had been to see an FA Cup game against Hornchurch, also from a lower league, and we'd lost. For that game, three years earlier, I had stood behind the goal that Bromley were (infrequently) attacking at the time. I didn't want to tempt fate by standing in the same place.

The stand was a big improvement since it had been rebuilt following the fire. For one thing, you didn't have to try to peer through about a dozen dirty or cracked panes of glass at the side, which were good for protecting you from the weather but a bit rubbish if you wanted to see what was happening on that half of the pitch.

The seats were a lot more comfortable, too. They had been bought from Wimbledon when they had left their Plough Lane ground. It was quite thrilling to think that the spectators who had previously sat on them had seen their team go all the way to Wembley, when their team won the FA Cup in 1988, beating Bruce Grobbelaar's Liverpool in the final. Was this yet another sign?

I wished Liz had decided to join me and share in the glory instead of choosing to spend the day in London, but her first and only visit to Hayes Lane hadn't been an unqualified success. She'd ended up playing Angry Birds on her phone, while Bromley went out of the FA Cup in that game against Hornchurch. Considering she was an American woman, whom I'd met in New Zealand, the chances of her developing a liking for English non-league football were never that high.

It was at this point that I discovered that I was sitting in front of a small clique of Didcot fans.

I knew this because a man directly behind me bellowed 'COME ON YOU DIDDYMEN!' at eardrum-shattering volume, which at least solved the question of their nickname. I looked around for an alternative, quieter place to sit and was distressed to see the stand was absolutely packed.

As I looked around, I spotted a few familiar faces. They were faces I'd only seen on Facebook but people who I had become Facebook friends with through a shared love of Bromley FC. I made a mental note to go and talk to them, but changed my mind when I realised that I couldn't remember any of their names.

There were also quite a few older supporters, which brought home to me the fact that I too was ageing. I could see my future – sitting in the stand, blanket draped over my lap, watching Bromley's continued rise. I was particularly looking forward to the blanket part of it – I was definitely feeling the cold more as I headed towards my sixties.

But although there were no seats to spare, at least I'd got a look at the shouty man. He was large and ruddy-faced, and looked to be in his early fifties, with greying hair poking out from beneath his red and white bobble hat. A similarly dressed woman sat next to him, right down to the hat. They both wore red and white scarves and had a blanket draped over their laps. Overhearing him (it wasn't difficult) offering up his expert opinion gave me even more confidence. It sounded as though this game, one of the biggest in their history, had come at a bad time for the Diddymen. Following relegation the previous season, the manager had walked out, players had left in droves and their budget had been slashed.

I almost felt sorry for them. Almost. Apparently they'd even gone to the trouble of preparing an extensive sixty-page dossier on Bromley before the game. But if this made them sound professional, the thought soon vanished when I got my first sight of them.

Most teams, in my experience, are led out by their captain when playing in the fourth qualifying round of the FA Trophy. Not Didcot. Leading them out of the tunnel was a man in his forties, with a huge gold chain around his neck and wearing a bright red coat. The Mayor of Didcot, no less, was fresh from his duties opening the Didcot charity fireworks display. The fact that he was at Hayes Lane was an indication, perhaps, that this was a bigger game for Didcot than it was for us. In fact, I suddenly realised with a warm glow that this was their Wembley – possibly the biggest game in their history.

The middle-aged Mayor looked in a lot better shape than some of the players. At least three of them were overweight, the sixteen-year-old looked more like a fourteen-year-old and the goalkeeper was so bad that he had once been 'let go' by

Bromley. I felt immense satisfaction knowing that the man behind me would not have much to shout about in the next ninety minutes.

As is often the case, the underdogs started well, but I wasn't worried. I'd seen it all before. Despite that, I definitely wasn't expecting what happened after about twenty minutes, when Alex Stanley, the only player of theirs I recognised (he'd scored for Yeading against Newcastle in the FA Cup) hit a sweetly timed volley, which sailed past Tommy Forecast, clipping the inside of the post on its way into the back of the net. Didcot Town were winning and the man behind me couldn't contain his joy.

'THAT'S THE WAY TO DO IT DIDDY, YOU'VE GOT THIS ONE!'

I tensed slightly on hearing this, even though what he was saying was laughable. Then I relaxed. He was just one of those eccentric types that non-league football always seems to attract. He was harmless enough. And the goal? I tried to see it for what it was – nothing more than an early consolation goal which I shouldn't begrudge them. I was still feeling confident and enjoying the game. Or at least I was until a loud bellow came from behind me ten minutes later.

'COME ON DIDDY, THIS LOT ARE A BUNCH OF USELESS PANSIES!'

Pansies? Pansies? No one said pansies any more. I was starting to get a bit irritated with him: a mixture of my jet lag and him being supremely annoying. I found myself looking forward to when Bromley scored, which would doubtless shut him up, and I didn't have long to wait.

A few minutes later, Hakeem Araba collided with ex-Bromley keeper Dean Santangelo on the edge of the area and the referee, after consulting his linesman, pointed to the spot. This enraged the already-quite-worked-up man behind me, so much so that his voice went up several octaves and sounded completely different.

'YOU ARE JOKING REF! HOW MUCH ARE THEY PAYING YOU?'

As I looked around, I saw that it wasn't him who had shouted this, but the almost identical-looking woman sitting next to him, who had disbelief written all over her face at the match official's decision. Since it was a blatant penalty in my eyes (apart from the offence having taken place slightly outside the area), I felt that justice had been done. As Danny Waldren tucked the spot kick away, I felt an extra layer of happiness. Not only were we back in the game but neither of the Didcot fans behind me seemed to have anything to say.

Shortly afterwards, Rory Hill came close to giving Bromley the lead when he had a shot cleared off the line, but it felt as though normal service was being resumed after the early set-back. Better still, there was the welcome sound of silence in the stand.

Then, just as half-time approached, and I was thinking long-ingly about Battenberg and tea, the unthinkable happened. Uche Ikpeazu, who was only there for work experience, saw Forecast off his line and chipped the ball over him from thirty yards out. It was one of the best goals I'd ever seen. And it wasn't just me who felt that way.

'YOU BEAUTY, UCKY LAD!' he screamed, while she was content with a simple, 'GET IN THERE!'

I sank into my seat. I was genuinely unable to process what was going on. Children scoring world-class goals against Bromley? Losing to a team that played in the Zamaretto League Division One South and West? Sitting behind a couple who were unknowingly crushing my spirit?

Half-time brought with it a further series of disappoint-ments. I already knew that there was unlikely to be any Battenberg in the new-style tea hut, but no biscuits either? What's the point of tea without cake or biscuits?

The programme had also undergone a huge transformation. No longer was it used as an outlet for disgruntled honorary secretaries to rant about named-and-shamed players not trying hard enough, clueless managers using poor tactics and supporters getting up to all sorts of things they didn't approve of.

No longer was it typed out on a couple of sheets of cheap paper by the honorary secretary himself and printed on a hand-cranked Gestetner machine he kept in the spare room at home, before he got his family to fold the programmes by hand. That entire process took place the night before a game, so the team news was as up to date as possible.

The modern-day programme was very slick and beautifully produced but wasn't quite the same. Not that this had stopped me from buying two and putting one straight into a Ziploc plastic bag for my collection.

When the players came back on, Bromley had rung the changes with subs replacing two of the more ineffective players, but nothing else had changed. The Didcot supporters' club behind me were keeping up their mixture of running commentary and the shouting of encouragement at their team.

Bromley looked more likely to score, with the manager's son Bradley Goldberg narrowly missing from just outside the box. But, after an hour, one of the overweight Didcot centre backs nodded home a powerful header from near the penalty spot and, unbelievably, we were 3-1 down. Could it get any worse?

Yes, it could. The woman behind me rubbed salt into the wound by shouting the most hurtful words she'd come up with all day.

'COME ON BROMLEY!' she screamed, 'MAKE A GAME OF IT!'

And then it all went even further and more rapidly downhill.

Danny Waldren, probably driven to an act of rashness by the voices from the stands, went in for a two-footed lunge on Didcot's Danny Seaward, who had been the best player on the pitch. The referee seemed to hesitate briefly, until a man's shout came from behind me.

'SEND HIM OFF, RADCLIFFE! RED CARD EVERY DAY OF THE WEEK!'

When the referee dutifully produced the red card, I was seething. Although impressed that the Didcot shouter had used the official's correct name, I was convinced that his demand had influenced the match official's decision.

Suddenly, I was overwhelmed with jet lag-induced tiredness and, at the same time, the life seemed to drain out of Bromley. I was just glad Liz hadn't come. I was having to put up with garbage from all sides – in front of me on the pitch and behind me in the stand. I had had enough. Didcot had even taken off three players at once, just to give their subs a run. And after that, they could have made it 4-1, but Forecast made a great save from Seaward. For the first time I could remember, I thought about leaving early, but decided it wasn't worth sacrificing my proud record of never having missed a minute of a Bromley game I'd watched, so forced myself to witness every last, sorry minute.

Determined not to let the people behind me have the final word, I turned around and glared at them and then, back facing the pitch, shouted at the Bromley players wandering off down the tunnel.

'COME ON BROMLEY!'

It just sounded weak and ineffective. It was too little, too late and my heart wasn't in it. Didcot had won. The people behind me had won. As I looked around one last time, I saw them giving their team a standing ovation. This only added to the pain.

I left my seat quickly, feeling flat, tired and wishing I'd

ignored those impossible-to-ignore signs. I'd been totally convinced that today would be a first step on the long road to Wembley. Instead, it was the end of the road for yet another season.

When I got back to the hotel, Liz told me that she'd spent the afternoon in bed, watching racing on TV. I felt slightly offended that she had somehow found that preferable to watching Bromley, but kept the thought to myself.

That night, struggling to stay awake, I watched *Strictly Come Dancing* for the first time. I'd read a lot about it, and it seemed hugely popular, so I was quite looking forward to seeing what all the fuss was about. But when Robbie Savage removed his trousers at the end of his dance, I decided it was time to go to sleep.

Two days later, I discovered that, not only had I missed out on a trip to Wembley, but I'd also been beaten by a better book in the William Hill Sports Book of the Year awards. But unlike the Didcot disaster, I hadn't been expecting a win and was genuinely happy to have made the shortlist. After the ceremony, I went to see my dad again as we were flying back to Boston the next morning. It was a shame I probably wouldn't be able to share the adventures of the day, but it felt like a bonus being able to spend time with him.

As I reached the reception desk, the nurse burst into a smile as soon as she saw me. 'Congratulations' was all she said. When I gave her a puzzled look, she said, 'Your dad is very proud of you.'

I still wasn't sure what she meant until I walked into his room and the first thing he said was that he'd heard me being interviewed on *Front Row* on BBC Radio 4 and had insisted on telling all the nurses and porters about it. He'd also asked one of them to cut out any articles about the award from the papers.

He seemed almost like his old self and asked me about the

interview, wanting to know what the interviewer was like. He seemed genuinely proud.

For once, I didn't care about having to wait a while longer to see Bromley at Wembley. This had made the whole trip worthwhile.

And besides, two seasons later, I was back. Although the last things I was expecting to see at Hayes Lane on my return were Minnie Mouse, a giant tent and half a dozen cheerleaders.

CHAPTER TWELVE

When a reserve midfielder left Bromley for Salisbury City just before the start of the 2014/15 season it made almost every national newspaper.

His name was Prince Khalid Bin Bader Alsaud and he was newsworthy due to being the first member of Saudi Arabian royalty to play professional football in England. He was a bit useless, apparently, and never got anywhere near making Bromley's first team. In fact, he'd only made the reserves a couple of times.

He'd been tempted to make the move to Wiltshire by Salisbury's new owner, Moroccan businessman Otail Touzar, who described himself as 'the youngest Club Owner/Chairman/ Head coach/Player in the World, an achievement that was never done before and will surely stand for many years to come.'

He told the *South West Business* website that he had been 'in negotiations' with several top Premiership or Spanish clubs to buy them, but had settled on Salisbury City, who played in the Skrill Conference Premier. Touzar persuaded the shareholders to sell the club to him for £1 by showing pictures of him-

Dave Roberts

self with Roman Abramovich, José Mourinho and Cristiano Ronaldo.

Prince Khalid Bin Bader Alsaud was Touzar's first signing, and Touzar told the *Western Daily Press* – exclusively – that he was in talks to bring a second big name, Niall Horan from boy-band One Direction, into the squad.

I'd often dreamed about a similar kind of investor coming into Bromley and throwing his money around on equally high-profile, but preferably much better, players. Which made it all the more exciting when that was exactly what happened.

Ashley Reading was a businessman, apparently with deep pockets, who was going to change things. He'd been appointed co-chairman with Jerry Dolke and was young, ambitious and dynamic. He illustrated the last quality by posting a video showing him bounding around Hayes Lane at high speed whilst talking (equally rapidly) about the changes that would be taking place during the Reading era.

The bar, which had taken the place of the tea hut, was being rebuilt. It was in the process of being transformed into a 'fantastic American style bar/restaurant with gourmet food, the latest craft beers and a charging station for iPhones.' Before that blast of modernity had a chance to sink in, he'd zipped off to his next destination – a huge 'multifunctional marquee' on the side of the ground. This, he explained breathlessly, would be a 'fantastic commercial business venture', hired out for events like antique and craft fairs as well as wine-tasting evenings.

Bromley were heading upmarket and Reading's enthusiasm was contagious. I found myself nodding along as he spoke. This was going to be brilliant. So brilliant, that I somehow managed to overlook some of the things that didn't quite feel right – like giving the Hayes Lane driveway 'a fantastic classy, country club feel', leading to an 'absolutely beautiful car park'.

135

He'd be putting in hedging, presumably to block out eyesores like the paddock and bowls club.

The club shop, meanwhile, was moving to a double-storey modular building near the entrance, which would also house the offices on the first floor. And there was more, much more, including artificial pitches and a kind of gourmet new-style tea hut that would sell everything from home-made soup to jacket potatoes.

Reading had a 'fantastic five-year plan', and it was starting right now.

Living in the US, I felt as though I was a million miles away from the exciting transformation of Hayes Lane. And although Liz and I had often talked about living in the UK, we'd never done anything about it.

I had to rely on the Bromley forum to keep up with the Reading revolution, but his vision was fast becoming reality. Only a week after his video, fans were talking about freshly potted flowers and shrubs lining the drive. There was soon talk of Family Fun Days. These featured things like a bouncy castle and face painting. There would be a new mascot, Billy Bromley, and Disney characters like Buzz Lightyear and Minnie Mouse wandering around Hayes Lane (or The Fortress, as it was now known) rubbing children's heads.

It was announced that Bromley goals would be greeted by loud music – specifically, 'Chelsea Dagger' by the Fratellis, a song that I had hated from the first time I heard it. Further loud music would be blasted from the tent and girls would roam the terraces wearing backpacks which dispensed lager (mainly to dads) through hand-held hoses. For further refreshment, the Ravens Bar and Grill was now open and on the menu were Bromley-themed meals, such as 'The Goldburger', named after manager Mark Goldberg. Did they also offer a Jamie Slabber-inspired 'Slabber Steak'? I hoped so.

The craters in the car park that I'd had to circumnavigate when I had a scooter were tarmacked over. And, on the field, Bromley were winning – we were 6/1 with the bookies to win promotion and, if you wanted a bet, you could place it through Bromley's new 'club betting service', called My Club Betting. These were heady days. This was football. But not as I knew it.

The FA Trophy qualifying round draw a few months later brought more good news – we would be away to newly relegated Tonbridge Angels. I followed the game on Twitter and it looked as though there was very little to tweet about – the game finished 0–0 and prompted a radical innovation of my own. Following a goalless draw on Twitter wasn't ideal, so I invented a whole new way to follow a Bromley match from the other side of the Atlantic, although it did require a little patience.

I'd noticed that, within a day of a match being played, high-lights would appear on YouTube. All I had to do was avoid the score and keep checking YouTube until the match highlights were posted. Then I'd watch the game, condensed into five or six minutes of highlights, as though I was there. It was a similar strategy to the one I had used for *Match of the Day* when I was growing up.

The first time I used it in the modern era was for the Tonbridge replay. The opening shot was a disappointment. I'd been expecting packed terraces, cheerleaders, Donald Duck and free-flowing lager being dispensed as fast as fans could drink it. Instead, the ground looked empty. Perhaps everyone was in the Ravens Bar and Grill tucking into their Slabber Steak.

The teams came out to the *Rocky* theme, which made a change from 'Yesterday' by the Merrymen or the brass-band version of 'Snoopy Versus the Red Baron' that Charlie King favoured before his Caribbean cruise.

Bromley soon took the lead, when Jerrome Sobers sliced the ball past his own keeper. This was followed by some equally rubbish football, with Bromley missing two open goals and blazing several shots over the bar. But the stress eased a bit when a penalty was given after Moses Ademola was tripped in the box. He picked himself up, tucked the ball away and it was 2–0. Jamie Slabber then got in on the act, scoring a third. 'Get in, Slabs!' said the cameraman and Bromley were safely through.

The draw for the next round was once again a kind one – we would be at home to Leiston, from the Ryman Premier League, who were in the first round for the first time in their history.

Delight was tempered by mutterings on the forum about budget cuts, which gave me a slightly uneasy feeling. The anxiety grew a few days later, when someone pointed out that Ashley Reading hadn't been seen around for a while. Despite this, the main discussion around the Leiston game seemed to be what the headline would be in the *News Shopper* if Bromley won.

'LAZY LEISTON SLAIN BY RAVENS' was the first suggestion, followed by two similar efforts: 'WIN IS THE LEIST RAVENS DESERVE' and 'BROMLEY'S LEIST LEIST SHOW'.

I was fairly sure none of these would be used.

On the Saturday that the game took place, I managed to avoid the result by forgetting it was on. By the time I remembered, the following morning, footage of it was already up on YouTube.

The pitch looked to be a typical early-December Hayes Lane mudbath and Leiston were soon on the attack, threatening to make the headlines look a bit premature. 'Oh blimey,' said the cameraman with relief, as a cross/shot hit the inside of home keeper Seb Brown's post.

That was followed by someone from Bromley scuffing a shot wide of the post, and someone else heading just over the bar. The players responsible were amongst those I hadn't yet learned to identify.

The game then deteriorated into a series of misses and hopeless attempts on goal, interspersed by a lucky Jamie Slabber tap-in ('Get in, Slabs!') after a fumble by the Leiston keeper to give Bromley the lead. If these were the highlights, I was glad I didn't have to see what went on in between them.

By this stage, the main entertainment came not from the on-field action, but from overhearing more of the cameraman's conversations. 'I had one, but I fell on it,' he said to someone, who laughed in reply. I was still trying to work out what it could have been that he had fallen on (I hoped it wasn't a hamster or something like that), when Bromley added a second goal. Moses Ademola lobbed the ball over a static Leiston defence and Louis Dennis, who was fast becoming my favourite player, ran on to it and scored.

The headline on the *News Shopper* website, when I perused it a few days later, read 'BROMLEY DUMP LEISTON OUT OF THE TROPHY'. That was the leist they could manage.

But Bromley were into the second round of the FA Trophy, and just four games away from Wembley. The draw, when it was announced, wasn't ideal: away to Torquay United, a well-established Football League side now plying their trade in the Conference, and a long way for the fans to travel. But Torquay would be a bit nervous too. Especially since Bromley were sitting in second place in the league (the Conference South) below them and Mark Goldberg had just been named Manager of the Month.

I was looking forward to this. It would be a good test of how far we'd come and, as it was such an important game, I decided to make watching it even more authentic by ordering a programme. This would mean having to stop myself watching the highlights until it arrived in the post.

It took six days for the programme to wing its way to Connecticut, which was, of course, far too late. I cracked as soon as the highlights appeared on YouTube just a few days after the game had taken place.

I'd successfully avoided the result and, as I sat down to watch the highlights on the laptop, I felt a familiar mix of excitement and hope. As the teams walked out onto the Launa Windows Stadium pitch, I noticed that the video, which had been posted by Torquay, was much shorter than the usual Bromley ones – it was only one and a half minutes long.

What did this mean? I decided that it had to be a good sign, possibly indicating a dreary, uneventful, goalless draw, with a replay to come at Hayes Lane. I'd take that.

But seconds into the video, as I was basking in the glow of this imaginary stalemate against a famous team who played at the highest level of non-league football, I had a ghastly realisation. I was watching goal highlights only.

After twenty-four seconds, Torquay scored with a lucky deflection. After forty-one seconds, they had gone two goals up, also with a lucky deflection. After fifty-six seconds, it was 3-0 with a goal that was slightly more deserved. And twenty-two seconds later, it was four. A minute and twenty-seven seconds after I'd started watching, the teams were shaking hands as they walked off the pitch. I was shell-shocked. It wasn't even two minutes ago that I had been full of hope and dreaming of Wembley. It had been brief and brutal.

But it turned out to be just what was needed. Mark Goldberg brought in a couple of players, including his son Brad (who had left for Bristol Rovers earlier in the season) and Anthony Cook. In another change, former Irish Under-23 international Alan Julian took over in goal. He was soon being compared with all-time Bromley favourite, Curtis Hayes (who had a reputation for being the nicest keeper ever, even apologising to the opposition if he saved anything).

These three joined several players who would have been considered far too good for Bromley when I used to watch them in person, like Rob Swaine as captain (when he signed, he had to pretend he wasn't limping, having bruised ligaments in his foot after leaping onto a boat in Marbella), Louis Dennis (who was just about the most skilful player ever to wear a Bromley shirt) and Moses Ademola (who would later change his name to Moses Emmanuel).

Hopes that this was finally going to be our Wembley season were never higher. And there was more good news. T. J. Herbert had been in regular contact and was still convinced he would be making a film of *The Bromley Boys*, despite the first round of fundraising bringing in a total of £125.50 towards a budget of around £750,000. He was getting a script written by someone he knew in Brighton and promised to send it to me as soon as it was ready.

But the most exciting news was that Reece Shearsmith, from *The League of Gentlemen*, had agreed to play Charlie King in the film. A few days later came the depressing news that Shearsmith hadn't agreed to play Charlie King after all – it had been a comedic misunderstanding between his agent and T. J. Undeterred, T. J. announced that Martine McCutcheon and Hugh Grant were being approached to play my parents – reuniting them for the first time since *Love, Actually*.

As well as that, a director who had worked with Gwyneth Paltrow was being lined up and Louis Tomlinson from One Direction (not to be confused with his bandmate Niall Horan, who was wanted by Salisbury City), was being looked at to play Bromley's star striker, Alan Stonebridge.

T. J. certainly thought big.

The same was true of Ashley Reading, but rumours were flying around that he had now left the club in mysterious circumstances. Someone had posted on the forum that the money he'd promised to invest in the club hadn't gone through, and that the builders of the Ravens Bar and Grill were on the verge of driving a JCB through it because they hadn't been paid.

His five-year plan had lasted a little over five months. By April, it was confirmed that Jerry Dolke was back in charge and that a consortium of fans had come on board to save Bromley from going under.

While it was true that the Ravens Bar and Grill had proved to be a big success, the club shop and offices never did get their brand-new, two-storey, modular building. Instead, they were permanently housed in Portakabins near the turnstiles.

And although Bromley didn't make the FA Trophy final (it was won by the virtually unknown North Ferriby United), at least they took part in the tournament, unlike Salisbury, who had the rare distinction of being banned. They were disbanded before the season had started, after chairman Touzar turned out to have been not entirely truthful when he claimed to be a successful businessman with links to oil-rich Saudis.

He was rumoured to have been sleeping in the Salisbury changing room, posing with expensive cars belonging to other people and holding training sessions at top-secret locations. His big signing, Prince Khalid Bin Bader Alsaud, never got around to playing as Touzar had ignored the fact that there was a transfer embargo imposed on Salisbury.

He still hadn't paid the £1 he owed as payment for the club.

Bromley, meanwhile, were in much better shape. Mark Goldberg was doing a great job as manager, Moses Ademola was scoring at will and Jerry Dolke had taken the club from the bottom of the Ryman League Premier Division to the verge of making history.

Bromley just needed a win at home to Weston Super Mare to seal promotion to the Conference and take their place amongst the elite of non-league football.

I took every measure humanly possible to avoid the score, as I waited for the highlights to appear on YouTube. This meant a self-imposed media blackout in case some globally newsworthy event had taken place at Hayes Lane – for example, a member of the Saudi royal family dramatically returning to the club and scoring the winning goal.

As a result, I stopped reading the paper and, every time the sports news came on TV, I would shut my eyes, stick my fingers in my ears and make a low humming sound to block out hearing any potential spoilers. Often for several minutes at a time, which Liz found extremely annoying. She didn't understand why I didn't just look up the result as soon as the game was over and save myself – and her – all the trouble.

Later that night, despite checking at least four or five times an hour, there was still nothing on YouTube. Had the game been postponed? Or perhaps the club were so gutted with the result that they couldn't bring themselves to post a video.

I couldn't really check any of these theories, in case I accidentally saw the score. But then, just as I was on the verge of cracking and looking up the result, a version finally showed up. It had been filmed from his seat in the stands by one of the fans, Paul Haughey, and was entitled BROMLEY FC PRO-MOTION – BROMLEY v WESTON SUPER MARE.

I was so filled with relief and joy that I didn't care about the huge spoiler in the title. The minute-and-a-half video started with the walk up the drive, which was lined with withering plants and dying cedar trees. It then cut to players warming up, as Hayes Lane slowly filled.

The first goal came from Reece Prestedge, finishing nicely from ten yards out. Then Brad Goldberg set Jamie Slabber up for a second and the crowd went absolutely berserk. After the final whistle, they ran onto the pitch and began the celebrations, dancing and singing with the players in front of the John Fiorini Stand.

And as if it couldn't get any better, the caption at the end read BROMLEY 3 WESTON SUPER MARE 0, so there'd been another goal not captured on camera.

I watched the short video over and over again. It was electrifying seeing the goals, the celebrations and Rob Swaine lifting the Conference South championship trophy. Despite appearing less than an hour ago, the video had already been seen 104 times, and at least fifteen of those were by me. The excitement pumping through me was mixed with a tinge of sadness that I'd had to watch it on my own, 6,000 miles away.

It was only later that the true significance of the result sank in. Bromley had won promotion to the Conference, which meant that we would now have THREE chances to get to Wembley each season – the FA Cup (highly unlikely), FA Trophy (a fair chance) and the Play-Offs (not impossible).

By coincidence, by the time the new season started, Liz and I were living in the UK.

CHAPTER THIRTEEN

Liz and I moved to Leeds just in time for Bromley's first season in what was now the newly renamed Vanarama National League. By the end of it, we'd finished fourteenth and I'd collected four non-league mugs.

The mug acquisition started in nearby Halifax, when I decided that collecting programmes alone wasn't sufficient to commemorate the most glorious time in the club's history.

I needed to supplement them with something readily available in all non-league club shops, and mugs won out over badges (too easy to lose), pens (Liz would almost certainly keep stealing them) and replica shirts (I'd never be able to bring myself to buy a Sutton shirt).

Midway through the following season, after visits to Wrexham, Fylde and Guiseley, the collection had grown to six. The time felt right to post a picture of the mugs on Twitter. I carefully arranged them on my bookshelf, crests facing the camera, and, in common with my programme collection, arranged in alphabetical order. They were all in pristine condition, and none had ever been drunk out of, to the best of my knowledge.

Although I wasn't totally happy with the photo (the glint

from the flash reflected on the mugs), I couldn't wait to post it, which I did straight away.

But while I was basking in the glory of dozens of likes, a tweet from Ian, a fellow Bromley fan, sent shockwaves of alarm through my body. His tweet simply showed a photo of at least fifteen non-league mugs lined up on his mantelpiece and heralded the beginning of a new and thrilling pastime – competitive non-league mug collecting.

I would often bump into Ian at away matches, both of us clutching a plastic bag containing the latest addition to our collections. By the time the 2017/18 season had got underway, I was stuck on twelve mugs and the fixture list showed few opportunities to add to that number.

Bromley's first season in the top flight of non-league football had provided me (and Liz on occasion – memorably so when I took her abroad, to Wrexham, for her birthday) with the perfect opportunity to reacquaint myself with my home country, to travel the length and breadth of the land and to write a book about it, *Home and Away*. All this travelling had eaten up the meagre book advance, so I was now limited for financial reasons to away games at northern grounds.

Of the current National League teams, North Ferriby and

Solihull Moors were the only clubs whose shops I hadn't yet visited. This was an added reason for wanting a good run in the FA Trophy – any draw away to a team in my part of the country would give me a new club to visit and a new mug to buy.

There were slightly more reasons to be cheerful about the *Bromley Boys* film. I'd seen the script and really liked it, despite the storyline veering wildly from the book's, including giving the fifteen-year-old me a girlfriend.

At fifteen, I was a boy who went on supporters' club coaches to non-league football matches, ate Weetabix-and-Marmite sandwiches and wore his sister's pale blue bobble hat. No one would expect someone like this to have a girlfriend. It didn't feel plausible, but I was happy to go along with this rewriting of history.

That was just as well, since filming had already taken place a few months ago. I went along to the set at Crockenhill FC for an afternoon, where I swanned around self-importantly, pointing out historical inaccuracies which no one was remotely interested in.

At least these days I took trains to non-league games rather than coaches. But the first game in the 2017/18 FA Trophy was away to Hartley Wintney and I wasn't sure if I'd be going because I had no idea where it was. I felt a burst of hope when I heard the draw – Hartley Wintney definitely sounded north-ern. Was it anywhere near me?

After googling it, I found, to my disappointment, that it was in Hampshire and had a population of 4,999, which immediately made me want to move there, just to round up the num-ber. Instead, I wouldn't even be visiting. I was broke and would have to miss out on what could well be the first step on the road to Wembley. I'd also be missing out on a mug that I was unlikely to get another chance to own.

The disappointment was diluted slightly when I discovered that BT Sport had sent a reporter along and would be getting regular updates from him. The reporter, when he made his first appearance after about twenty minutes, struggled to find anything to say about the game, other than that nothing had happened so far.

I was following the game on Twitter at the same time, and the first piece of disappointing news was that Ian was there. And, distressingly, he'd tweeted the Hartley Wintney club shop on the way to the ground to see if they sold mugs. My heart sank when they replied that they did. This would extend his five-mug lead to six.

The BT reporter, whose face was a Trump-esque shade of orange, was still having trouble finding anything to talk about. It was such an uneventful game that he can't have been far off updating viewers on the latest news from the world of competitive non-league mug collecting.

But eventually, with time running out, Josh Rees put Bromley ahead and then George Porter, who had been so annoying when playing for Leyton Orient, but was fast becoming a Hayes Lane favourite, made it 2-0. Bromley were through to the second round.

I listened to the draw live on talkSPORT, desperately hoping for an away game in the north and, for once, the football gods were smiling at me. We'd be visiting Blyth Spartans, from the Conference North.

Blyth had a scary record in knockout competitions and were current holders of the Debenhams Cup, even though they had last won it in the late 1970s. That's because everyone lost interest in it after that.

This wasn't hugely surprising – the Debenhams Cup was played for by the two teams from outside the top two divisions who got furthest in the FA Cup. Blyth Spartans had become giant-killing legends at this time, culminating in them reaching the fifth round of the Cup in 1977/78 and attracting a crowd of more than 42,000 to Newcastle's St James's Park in the process.

The only reason I liked the Debenhams Cup was because The Grubby worked for Debenhams at the time. This gave me what I felt to be a personal connection to the trophy.

The Grubby was a porter in the carpet department, which was probably the best job on the planet, apart from general manager of Bromley FC. There were never any customers and all he had to do was carry the occasional carpet from the storeroom to the showroom. The rest of the time was spent lounging around on a pile of rugs, smoking, drinking tea and reading the papers. I kept hoping he'd resign because he was bored and I'd be able to take his job, but it never happened.

And now, around forty years later, I was on my way to the home of the Debenham Cup holders, Blyth Spartans, as they took on Bromley. I was getting a lift from Jon, a fellow exile who also lived in West Yorkshire. His young son Dennis, who had inherited his dad's love for Bromley, was in the back.

Getting to Blyth early meant there was time to visit the beach, which came as a surprise to me as I had no idea Blyth was anywhere near the sea. Another unexpected bonus was the quality of chips on sale at one of the cafés where we all bought lunch. As we took them back to the car, I noticed the return of an old foe. Seagulls had blighted previous seasons' visits to Southport, Grimsby and Dover by circling me in a threatening manner, and they were back. But this time I was ready for them. I quickly finished my chips before they had a chance to swoop. As did Dennis.

Jon wasn't so cautious. He carelessly put his chips on the roof of the car while he unlocked the door. By the time he'd done that, the seagulls were already helping themselves.

As we drove the short distance to Croft Park, Jon, for reasons I couldn't quite fathom, was asking Dennis quick-fire questions about his age.

'When's your birthday?'

'May.'

'Right. And what year were you born?'

'2006. No, 2007.'

'Try again.'

'2008?'

'Great. So how old are you?'

Dennis furrowed his brow in concentration.

'Nine?'

'Brilliant. Good lad.'

This only added to my confusion. Dennis looked much older than nine. Nearer eleven or twelve. I only worked out what was happening after Jon parked outside Blyth Smartens, a barber's shop done out in the club colours of green and white, and we crossed the road to the ground. That was when I saw the admission prices, and suddenly it all made sense. At the bottom of the sign by the turnstile, it read: 'FREE ENTRY FOR UNDER 10s.'

Dennis got in without being interrogated and we got our first look at the Croft Park ground. It was a beautiful sight, a classic non-league ground: compact and with a small crowd scattered around all four sides.

We soon met up with the rest of the Bromley fans – around twenty or thirty in total. I looked around and there was a notable absentee. Ian hadn't made the trip. Much as I liked him, this was superb news. I'd never been happier not to see someone.

One person who was there, as expected, was David Gregory; he was a big, friendly man in his late forties, who had the same name as the Bromley goalkeeper. This was no coincidence, however, since he was his dad. And as supportive dads go, you couldn't ask for better. David toured the country in a camper van, with various family members, watching his son play, and had never missed a game. He went through agony every time, living every minute and usually looked exhausted by the final whistle.

When I saw him at Blyth, I mentioned that I'd heard about a save his son had made against Fylde the previous week. David got his phone out and played footage of the save several times.

After that, I dragged myself away, as there was somewhere I needed to go. The Blyth Spartans club shop. I walked in and looked around for the mug that would close the gap between Ian and me. At first glance, I couldn't see any, but it was a reasonably big shop and there wasn't a club shop in the country that didn't sell mugs. I asked the woman behind the counter and she told me that they were out of stock.

I stood there, gaping in disbelief. It was like I'd been presented with an open goal and had fluffed it.

'We've got some nice glasses though,' she said, indicating some small wine glasses with a bright green Blyth Spartans badge printed on them.

My heart sank, in double disappointment at this. Glasses were no mugs. Plus, I'd been in the north-east for over an hour and no one had called me 'pet' yet.

In the end, I bought a glass on the off chance that it would count as a legitimate non-league mug. Ian and I had both bought mugs at Rochdale in the FA Cup game earlier in the season. Although they were clearly Football League mugs, the rules of competitive non-league mug collecting seemed quite flexible and, since Ian and I had both bought one, they were allowed to count.

I didn't fancy my chances with the Blyth Spartans glass, but at least the programme would qualify for my collection. I had got into the habit of buying just one these days, on economic grounds, and had a quick flick through it.

As soon as I saw they'd included a picture of a load of Bromley fans, including me, ego won out over discipline and I went and bought a second programme. It felt comforting slipping back into old habits.

The highlight of the programme (apart from the picture, obviously) was a lengthy two-page history of Bromley 'from 1892 – Present', which abruptly stopped in 2005, presumably because they had run out of space. This was especially annoying as the last couple of years had been the best in the club's history. The current squad was stronger than ever, with no obvious weaknesses, which wasn't something I'd been able to say at any time in the previous fifty years.

The manager, Neil Smith, who had taken over from Mark Goldberg (Smith had previously been his assistant, in which role his duties had included writing the programme notes) was proving a smart choice. This was his third season in charge and each season he'd made history by achieving Bromley's best-ever finish.

I almost felt a small hint of optimism.

This was soon banished when Blyth made a strong start and Gregory was forced into a good diving save, much to his dad's delight.

It was a grey, overcast day (the floodlights were already on before the game kicked off) with an icy wind blasting into the faces of Bromley's fans behind the Spartans' goal. Snow was piled up against the advertising boards directly in front of us and I soon found myself wishing I'd worn a few more jumpers. If I'd known Blyth was on the coast, I probably would have done.

Several of the Bromley players wore gloves, although none of the Blyth team seemed to think this was necessary. Even in extreme conditions, gloves were a sight you rarely saw with northern teams, and only goalkeepers wore them. And that was probably reluctantly.

As I was thinking about gloves, and feeling grateful for my official Bromley FC black and white woollen mittens, which Jim from the club shop had talked me into buying, Bromley took the lead. Josh Rees scuffed his first effort from a few yards out, but reacted well to place the ball between the Blyth keeper's legs. There are few better sights in life than seeing your team score when you're standing directly behind the goal.

This was followed soon after by a second, when a defensive mistake allowed glove-wearing Louis Dennis to sweep the ball into the unguarded green and white net. Suddenly, a win seemed like an outside possibility.

At half-time I went to the bar, where I'd arranged to meet Mark, the Blyth-supporting editor of my favourite football magazine, *The Football Pink*. After a pleasant, and warm, break, it was back out for the second half.

Bromley continued to attack. Brett Williams hit the bar, and then Louis Dennis, who I had become convinced was one of the greatest-ever Bromley players, crossed for Rees to get his second and it was 3-0.

The pain of missing out on a Blyth Spartans mug was all but forgotten in the excitement of taking such a convincing lead. But a stressful final ten minutes was set up when Greg Rutherford beat David Gregory (Junior) from close range, to the visible angst of David Gregory (Senior), to make it 3-1.

Deep into injury time came the highlight of the match. Louis Dennis (who else?) cut in from the right and curled a perfect dipping shot into the top corner. His celebration was muted; it was as though he expected to score goals like that. He probably did – he'd scored a similar, but even better, one against Barrow on Non-League Day in 2015 – which got my vote for Goal of the Season in the *Two-Footed Tackle* fanzine poll.

The whistle went shortly after the goal and Bromley had beaten the Debenhams Cup holders 4-1, on their own ground. It wasn't as straightforward as the scoreline suggested, but more straightforward than I'd been expecting.

As we left the ground, I made a point of thanking the security woman standing by the gate. 'Have a safe journey home,' she said. Much to my disappointment, there was no 'pet' added at the end.

On the way back to Leeds, we stopped off at the Angel of the North sculpture, something I'd always wanted to see and, more importantly, take a selfie in front of.

It was huge, way bigger than I'd expected, with a wider wingspan than a Boeing 757. Posing with the Angel in the background was tough, as it was so dark that I couldn't see it. I took loads of pictures in the hope that one would turn out well. When I got back to the car I looked through them and, in every one, I looked like a startled rabbit against a background of darkness. Why didn't they light it up at night?

It had been a double north-east fail, adding to not being addressed as 'pet'.

When I got home, Liz was hard at work on a presentation. A friend of a friend had started up some kind of insurance company in London and was keen to talk to her about managing their social media. She'd talked to him on the phone and he wanted her to come down to the capital early the following week. Even though the train would cost over £100, which we could ill afford, it definitely seemed worth it. Liz spent the next few days working on the presentation, which looked fantastic.

She went down to London and was full of excitement when she got back. The CEO had painted a golden vision of the future of the company and his enthusiasm seemed contagious.

It was only a matter of when, and not if, she was offered the job. In the meantime, he often got in touch with her to discuss strategies.

After a couple of weeks, she was getting a bit worried that she hadn't heard from him and left him a message. He rang straight back, apologising for the delay, and assured her that he'd soon be able to confirm when she'd be starting.

And that was the last time she ever heard from Ashley Reading.

Meanwhile, Reading's old club, Bromley, were through to the third round of the FA Trophy. Amongst the big teams already out of the competition were Tranmere, Macclesfield and Hartlepool, who had all fallen victim to acts of giant(ish)-killing. If we got a good draw, there was a possibility we could have a decent run.

As I sat down to listen to the draw on the radio, I tried to prepare myself for disappointment. I told myself that it was unlikely I'd get what I craved – another away tie against a lowly rated northern team with a club shop that sold mugs.

But I got that and more. Much more.

I would be going to an FA Trophy game that I had fantasised about when I was in my early twenties. We'd drawn a team who had represented impossible glamour to me in those days.

We were away to Workington.

CHAPTER FOURTEEN

I don't think I'd ever felt more nervous before a Bromley game than
I did on the train to Workington. It wasn't so much the prospect of
crashing out of the FA Trophy to a side from the Evo-Stik League
who had recently attracted a crowd of eighty-one, but the prospect
of going across the Ribblehead Viaduct.

I do not like heights and even looking at photos of the viaduct
filled me with terror. It was a very high, narrow, flimsy-looking
bridge which, considering it had been built about 150 years ago,
was clearly on the verge of collapsing, probably just as our train was
crossing.

'Let me know when we're about to come to the viaduct,' I asked
Pete, a Leeds-based Bromley fan I was travelling with. Pete had an
encyclopaedic knowledge of most things, including viaducts, canal
locks, non-league football grounds and Eastern European lagers
(especially Perla from Poland and Bergenbier from Romania). I
wanted to prepare myself for the crossing by shutting my eyes in
plenty of time.

'That was it back there,' he said, finishing off his pot of Tesco
Peri Peri Chicken Pasta and washing it down with Irn Bru.

Was he talking about the snow-covered dip we'd just been

through? I'd spent years avoiding the Ribblehead Viaduct and it turned out to be nothing but a shallow valley.

The relief I felt was enormous and it meant I could move on to my next major worry. I'd arranged to meet a Workington fan for lunch before the game, at a venue Pete would have approved of – Tesco.

I was undecided about meeting the fan until I saw that (a) he was offering to pay and (b) he signed himself off as 'Gary, an avid Dave Roberts books fan'.

We met at Workington station and walked to Tesco, which was just a couple of minutes from the ground. I couldn't help noticing that we were being shadowed by Stu and Ben, Bromley fans we'd met up with at Carlisle. They had appointed themselves as my security detail, wanting to make sure that Gary was legit.

Stu and Ben seemed satisfied as we went into Tesco, and walked back towards the station to rejoin the Bromley contingent.

I'd never eaten at Tesco before. My nine-year-old grandson Zac's favourite restaurant was Morrisons, but I was happy to try something new. I quite like meeting up with opposition fans before a game, as it helps me get to know a bit about the team we're playing. Gary was a pleasant, easy-going man in his thirties who was completely in love with Workington AFC.

The only thing I knew when I looked at the menu on the wall behind the counter was that I had to have chips. I'd worked out that there was a definite link between my having chips for lunch during the Trophy run and Bromley winning.

Lunch was a fairly typical meeting of non-league fans talking before a game, each of us keen to out-gloom the other with predictions. We were both totally convinced our teams would lose. I asked him which Workington players to look out for and he named two, Scott Allison and Conor Tinnion. When he asked the same question, I listed seven, including Louis Dennis, Jack Holland and

Adam Mekki. I wasn't trying to intimidate him; I was just being indecisive.

He did say that a few clubs they'd played recently had complained about the state of the pitch, which he thought wasn't as bad as they made out. We then talked about programmes – I was keen to see Workington's, but he said that I shouldn't get my hopes up; it was good but not great.

As I finished my chips and glanced towards the clock, it was time to head towards the ground.

'Anything else I can tell you?' he asked as I got up.

'Do they sell mugs?'

He looked a bit confused and pointed to a man in a Tesco uniform who was restocking one of the shelves.

'I'd think so – he'll probably know. Shall I ask him?'

It seemed too complicated to explain that I was trying to find out if the Workington club shop sold mugs, as I didn't want to look like some kind of sad non-league fan who collected mugs. Competitively.

Outside the ground was a sign that read 'SANDWITH ROOF-ING, SUPPORTING NEXT HOME GAME. BROMLEY'. I still felt a big thrill seeing our name at grounds better known for hosting matches in the Football League. I remembered the time when I used to dream about drawing Workington in a cup competition. And now it had finally happened.

There was another reason for getting excited. My hero, George Best, had once captained Workington at the ground I was about to enter. The fact that he had been nearly forty at the time and the game was a friendly against a Lancashire League eleven didn't matter.

After I passed through the turnstiles, one thing was immediately obvious. The pitch was much worse than Gary had let on. It was muddy, scuffed up and waterlogged, with puddles everywhere. It reminded me of some of the grounds I'd played at in the Orpington and Bromley District Sunday League. If I'd known how bad it was, my predictions would have been even gloomier.

But at least the Workington fans were welcoming and friendly. Wearing a Bromley scarf meant getting stopped every few steps and asked if I'd had a good trip. I'd never experienced anything like it.

When I finally got to the club shop, I saw what I'd come for. A Workington mug. I'd seen about twenty Bromley fans and Ian wasn't among them. I didn't want to get my hopes up. I was pretty sure the club were running a coach, and that hadn't arrived yet.

The mug was good, easily up to the standard I had come to expect. It was the first I'd bought that resisted the standard white interior and coloured it red, to match the handle. I'd started taking a keen interest in club crests and Workington's consisted of seemingly random elements thrown together, including a unicorn with an anchor in its mouth and an ancient Roman holding what looked to be an electric lawnmower, although that couldn't have been right. Considering half their ground was underwater, it would have been a huge health-and-safety risk.

Despite the questionable crest, this was a mug that was going to take pride of place in my collection.

As I stood in the queue, I half thought about buying their entire stock of mugs just to make sure Ian couldn't get one, but then thought better of it. Liz generally got a bit grumpy when I came home with one non-league mug, let along twenty identical ones.

When I got out of the shop, Ian was on his way in. I froze when I saw him, but forced a smile – we both did. Ian had made an eight-hour train journey to get here; he'd bought his train ticket in advance, before the coach was announced. He gave me the team news, and it wasn't good. Louis Dennis (flu) and Adam Mekki (ankle), our two most exciting players, hadn't made the trip.

When the teams ran out, it was noticeable how small the

Workington players were alongside Bromley's. It looked like a Fathers v Sons game on a school sports day.

In keeping with the undersized theme, the dugouts seemed a lot smaller than I was used to, and looked ill-equipped for the extended personnel of the modern professional game. Were these standard size at this level?

The only thing I knew about Northern Premier League dugouts was that there was enough space in Mossley AFC's for Jason Hart of Clitheroe FC to 'enjoy sexy times with an unknown blonde' after a 4-1 loss a few seasons before. He was caught, track pants around his ankles, when someone filmed the encounter and posted it on Twitter. (That game, incidentally, had been billed as 'Ladies Day' in a bid to attract more female supporters.)

But back to the present day, and those in the Workington dugout must have felt considerable excitement in the first minute, when Conor Tinnion – who I'd been warned about – forced David Gregory Junior into a smart save. While David Gregory (Senior) enjoyed it, his son seemed to be suffering even more than usual, what with the uneven bounce and slippery, wet conditions.

Workington were adapting a lot better than we were and, shockingly, took the lead when their diminutive fullback swept home.

We were 1-0 down and the pitch was cutting up badly, making it impossible for Bromley to play their normal free-flowing passing game. As the minutes ticked away, the atmosphere at the Bromley end was getting increasingly miserable. There had to be gloomier places to go out of the FA Trophy, but I couldn't think of any. The drizzle had turned into a downpour from the dark, slate-grey sky. The only tiny consolation was that it made a great Instagram post.

The feeling amongst the supporters was that we were finished. There was talk of the Trophy being meaningless and that it was great that we could concentrate on the league.

But with ten minutes left and all hope long gone, Frankie Raymond crossed the ball and Jack Holland, so often the Bromley hero, lost his marker to glance the ball home from the edge of the six-yard box.

The small crowd behind the goal went berserk. Someone even started singing 'We're going to Wembley', but he was soon shushed. Why would you want to jinx it? It was far too soon to mention the W-word. The football gods frown upon such behaviour.

The final whistle went and we'd somehow got away with a draw. There was just enough time to clap the players off the field before everyone ran towards the exit. The one and only train to Carlisle, for the connection south to London, left twenty minutes after the end of the match.

When we got to Workington station, I saw several Bromley fans gathered around a poster looking distraught. Had the one and only train back to Carlisle been cancelled?

It was worse than that.

'NO ALCOHOL PERMITTED,' it said, followed by the confusingly worded 'NOBODY LIKES A DRUNK TRAIN'. Underneath, to make sure the message was getting across, were the words: 'DO NOT TAKE ALCOHOL ON BOARD. THIS IS A DRY TRAIN'.

It was a much quieter journey back to our respective homes than usual. Pete got his phone out to see the other FA Trophy results and announced with glee that Sutton had lost to Brackley Town, who-ever they were. Not only were the team we all hated with a passion out of the Trophy, but they had been knocked out by a team few people had heard of.

I had rarely seen Pete so happy. He went onto Twitter to find out more details about the game, but for some reason couldn't access the official Sutton feed. He eventually gave up, presuming there were technical problems, and said he'd try again later.

It wasn't just Pete's least-favourite team that had been knocked out that afternoon. Dover, one of the only other teams I actively dis-liked (a grudge that had started when they once refused to sell me a programme), had lost at home to Leyton Orient.

It was turning into a very good day for us both. But there was a sting in the tail of all this positive news. 'With Sutton and Dover out, we're the highest-ranked team left,' Pete pointed out. That was it. We were doomed. First people had started using the W-word and now we were favourites to win the FA Trophy.

At Carlisle station, we met up with the Bromley players, who had travelled there by coach. When I saw Jack Holland, I could only think of one word to say to him after his late goal. I said 'Thanks'.

When Pete and I got to Manchester, there was a bit of a wait for the Leeds train, so Pete decided to try the Sutton Twitter feed again. And again, he failed. But this time, he worked out why. The previous weekend, in a drunken anti-Sutton rage, he'd blocked them on Twitter. As I looked at the screen of people he'd blocked, I noticed that Sutton were far from the only ones. Others to have suffered from Pete's wrath included Paul Jarvis, John Legere and Time to Break. None of these were names I recognised, but Pete clearly had something against them. But now he seemed happy to finally read the Sutton feed.

When I got home, I removed the Workington mug from my backpack and went to the bookshelf to add it to the collection. That was when I noticed that the other mugs had been slightly rearranged – alternate mugs had been brought to the front, while the ones on either side had been pushed back, giving an 'in out' pattern. Liz had either got bored or was embracing my new-found passion. I asked her. She confirmed that she'd been bored.

The next day, I decided to watch the game again, something I often did as long as we hadn't lost. A couple of young Workington fans had filmed it and posted the highlights on YouTube. Their comments and conversations throughout the game were occasionally audible, which greatly added to the entertainment. They sounded as though they were around twelve and fifteen respectively, and it was fascinating seeing everything through the eyes of the other team's fans.

There were the predictable cries of 'Ref!', 'Penalty!' and 'Yellow card – diving!', together with the odd unusual insult, such as 'They can't even sit on their own bench!'

When Workington went ahead, the younger one was delirious. 'Look at the scenes!' he screamed, as the home fans celebrated, 'Just LOOK at the scenes!'

A short while later, after his team came close to adding a second, he shouted an encouraging 'Unlucky, son!' to the player whose shot had gone narrowly wide. A squeaky-voiced twelve-year-old calling a grown man 'son' took a bit of getting used to.

And when the crowd size was announced, the boys were beside themselves. 'What an attendance! 890!' said the older one, bursting with pride, while his younger friend contented himself with singing '890, 890'. As the game came close to its end, with Workington still in the lead, he shrieked 'This party just got started!'

Predictably, the late equaliser, which had given me so much relief, had the opposite effect on these two. There were no words from either of them as Jack Holland powered his header home.

My heart went out to the older boy at the end, when he had finally regained the power of speech. He let out a huge sigh and said, 'Awwww, noooo! I don't wanna replay, mon.' The pain in his voice was there for all to hear. I would have told him that it could have been a lot worse – at his age, I'd had to watch my team lose 9–0 at Sutton.

I wanted to put my arm around him and tell him everything would be all right. He would get used to the constant disappointments and he'd learn to relish the small triumphs. But that would have been bad advice. What I really wanted to tell the boys was that it wasn't too late to change their minds about supporting a non-league team. Go for one of the big Premier League clubs instead, someone like Manchester City, Chelsea or Liverpool.

That way, you'd never have to know the pain of losing your goalkeeper to a side several levels below, just because a rich owner had taken over. You'd never experience losing your star player for an important game because he couldn't get time off work. And you'd never suffer sleepless nights on transfer-deadline day, wondering if your best player was about to be snapped up by some glamorous League Two side.

And you'd never find yourself trawling the Internet to see if you could find commentary on an FA Trophy replay that few people seemed to care about, which is what I found myself doing. Luckily, my efforts were rewarded. BBC Radio Cumbria were covering the game live.

As part of my preparation for the replay, I went to the Workington forum, and soon learned that five of their first-teamers were unavailable. Most of these had jobs and wouldn't be able to get time off, especially at such short notice. The bench would be full of kids, apparently. And the other disadvantage Workington had was that they faced a 700-mile round trip.

I was still nervous, but the nerves lessened after a couple of minutes when Brandon Hanlan, on loan from Charlton, put Bromley ahead. Then, much to the commentator's delight, Workington equalised, with a 'well-taken effort from the edge of the area'. Things seemed quite even until (and I was having to rely on possibly biased opinion) a slightly flukey cross/shot towards the far post from Louis Dennis found the net and put Bromley 2-1 ahead.

In the second half, it seemed as though Workington simply ran out of steam. George Porter made it 3-1 and, in the last twenty minutes, it sounded like shooting practice. Four more goals followed, with Dennis, Wannadio, Higgs and Holland getting their names on the scoresheet.

It was only when Bromley went 7-1 up just before the end that it hit me. We were just two minutes away from the FA Trophy quarter-finals. Those two minutes passed slowly.

Then it was over. The Workington manager, Lee Andrews, was interviewed on the radio after the game and, after finishing his slice of pizza, said that they had just been unlucky to run into a class side like Bromley. As if that didn't make me feel good enough, he then said that Louis Dennis and George Porter were the difference. 'That Dennis,' he said, 'our lads didn't know where he was half the time.'

And then, media duties over, he got on the coach that would get them home by six in the morning. Some of the players were going straight to work.

When I checked on the forum the next day, there was further evidence that Workington fans were the nicest ones around. Who praises the referee after their team lose 7-1? Workington fans, that's who. 'A very decent ref,' said one. They were also full of admiration for Bromley and Neil Smith, saying that we deserved promotion and that they hoped we went on to win the Trophy.

I just hoped the two boys whose comments had made re-watching the first game so special weren't among the sixty or so Workington fans to have made the trip. I'm not sure they would have ever got over such a heavy defeat at such a young age – I speak from experience.

The draw for the quarter-final looked quite kind – a home tie against Spennymoor from the league below us. I had no idea that it would turn out to be the most shambolic football fixture I'd ever experienced.

CHAPTER FIFTEEN

Liz and I were stretched out on sunloungers by an oversized pool in a gated community in Florida. Her aunt, who lived there, had treated us to a fortnight's holiday and the weather conditions were ideal, with clear blue sky, sun beating down and a warm breeze blowing through the gently swaying palm trees.

Liz had quickly adjusted to the lifestyle of having a fresh gin and tonic (with ice and lemon) brought to her the second she finished the previous one. I felt that I was adapting less well. While everyone around me sported a deep tan, I was smothered in SPF50, which meant I was the palest person there, apart from a few angry red streaks in the areas where I'd omitted to apply sunblock.

And while everyone around me was wearing either brightly coloured Hawaiian beach shirts or brightly coloured bikinis, I was wearing a white Bromley home shirt and oversized khaki shorts.

The other major difference was that, while everyone around the pool seemed relaxed, either reading or chatting, I had tension etched all over my face as I stared at my phone. I was following Twitter coverage of the FA Trophy quarter-final between Bromley and Spennymoor Town, a task made harder by the erratic phone signal, which would often drop out for what felt like minutes at a time.

It was my fault I was in Florida and not at a cold and windy Hayes Lane. My planning had been poor. When I'd booked the holiday, I'd obviously consulted the Bromley fixture list, and it looked as though the only game I'd have to miss was Tranmere away (I'd already been there, done that, got the mug). I'd assumed that we'd have been knocked out of the Trophy by February. Like we always were.

But I was wrong. And a favourable draw meant that we now had a chance to get to the semi-finals without facing another team from the National League. I doubted that there would ever be a better chance for Bromley to get to Wembley.

Even though it was only ten in the morning in Florida, I'd already had a bowl of chips (or French fries, as the waiter called them). This was because the link between my eating chips before a Trophy game and Bromley winning was now established beyond any reasonable doubt. I was satisfied that I'd done all I could to help the team. It was now up to them.

By half-time, chances had been few and far between and, the longer Bromley went without scoring, the more unbearable the stress became. In order to prevent myself staring at the screen for the full ninety minutes, waiting for news, I frequently jumped into the pool, swam a width, got out, dried myself and only then allowed myself to check the score.

Deep into the second half it was still 0-0. It sounded as though the Spennymoor keeper, Dan Lowson, was having the game of his life. This was confirmed by the following Twitter post, which greeted me after swimming my fifth width of the day. It read:

84 | SAVE! Lowson pulls off an incredible save to deny Bromley the lead here. He got down well to his right to pluck the ball off the line and away from danger.

Thanks mainly to Lowson, the game finished scoreless. Normally, this would have been a massively depressing result, and would have ruined the rest of the day, but I had mixed feelings about it, since I'd be back in time for the replay the following Tuesday. Not only was the County Durham town of Spennymoor only an hour and a half away from home but Dan, a Bromley fan who lived in the same West Yorkshire village as me, Menston, messaged me to say that he'd be driving to the game and offered me a lift.

I couldn't wait to get home and just hoped Bromley would be able to find a way past Lowson. I had checked out the highlights on YouTube and, in my mind, his eighty-fourth-minute save was up there with that Gordon Banks stop from Pelé in the 1970 World Cup (as with Vic Lindsay against St Albans, this seemed to be my major point of reference for all-time world-class goalkeeping). And not only did Lowson save goals, he also scored them, having netted an eighty-yard free kick in a recent FA Cup game. He celebrated by attending a horseshoe-fitting competition the following day, which struck me as about as northern an activity as you could get. (Previously, this record had been held by the Salvation Army band playing 'Once in Royal David's City' while huddling for cover from a torrential rainstorm when Guiseley had hosted Bromley in a fixture which defined the home and away season for me.)

It seemed as though Dan Lowson was the one man standing between Bromley and a place in the semi-finals of the FA Trophy. But there was bad news waiting for me when I got back home. The game had been postponed due to the Spennymoor pitch being waterlogged and had been rescheduled for the following Tuesday.

At least this gave me the chance to get over the jet lag

and, on the morning of the rearranged game, a local referee inspected the pitch and announced that it was playable. The replay would go ahead.

To help prepare for it, I went to the Spennymoor website, where they had 'Five Facts about Bromley FC'. I soon wished I hadn't bothered.

The fifth fact was called 'Reading Material'. I was initially excited to see my picture there and started to see what they had to say. It began with the unflattering (but sadly true) words 'Dave Roberts. A name which might not ring any bells when it comes to famous authors...'. I gave up after that.

There was still time before Dan arrived to check out the Spennymoor mug on the club shop's website, and it was a thing of beauty, with the club crest – something to do with lions, swords and suits of armour – on the front. I couldn't wait to get my hands on it.

And I wouldn't have long to wait because we were soon on the way to the Brewery Field, Spennymoor. Dan's car was a small one, a Ford Focus. He was in the front with Lloyd, a York-based Bromley fan, while I was in the back with Ben, a Cardiff-based Bromley fan. It felt slightly cramped, due to Dan and Lloyd both being six foot five and, frankly, seemingly even more enormous than that. I was just grateful that Ben had managed to lose something like twelve stone in the past year, otherwise it could have been an even tighter squeeze. But I didn't really care. We were on our way to the biggest Bromley game in many years.

And we weren't the only ones. According to Twitter, there were around twenty Bromley fans making their way to Spennymoor: Tim Wheeler had left at 9.30 in the morning and was driving up with Ian the mug collector; there were Uncle Gary and Dingle Dangle ('The Spennymoor Four are on the way'); while the Weavers – three generations of Bromley women from the same family – were also making their way there by car and had left a little earlier ('The Spennymoor Three might make it before you'). Another fan called Dan had already arrived and tweeted a picture of himself at the ground. It looked fairly empty, but there was still around an hour before kick-off. The Bromley team and management had also made the long journey on the day, catching a train from Euston at 10.30 a.m.

Excitement was building. Although no one in Dan's Focus actually used the W-word, there was a definite awareness that, if we managed to win tonight, we would be in the semi-final of the FA Trophy. And if we won that, we would be playing at the W-word. There was already concern that the club had jinxed things by tweeting that we were 'Three games from Wembley'. Madness.

As we saw the first road signs showing we were entering Spennymoor, Lloyd held up his phone and announced in a matter-of-fact voice, 'Game's off, boys'. There was a collective groan once we realised he was serious. He then read the tweet, which said 'The match referee has deemed the pitch water-logged and unsafe.' How could this happen? The pitch had been inspected that morning and passed. The players and management had already arrived at the ground. Fans, some of whom were making a 600-mile round trip, were just arriving.

One fan, who refused to be denied his Bromley fix, immediately set off back down the A1 to catch the clash between Knaresborough Town (who had someone called Bromley in their line-up) and Armthorpe Welfare.

We decided to take the softer option. Since the Brewery Field ground didn't have a clubroom, most people used a local pub and that was where we headed.

As soon as we arrived, we walked through a crowd of Spennymoor supporters, who were equally unimpressed that the game had been called off. I asked a couple if the club shop would be open and they said that they doubted it was – but one did confirm that they sold mugs. I'd pick one up when we returned which, if rumour was to be believed, would be on the following Tuesday night.

I then noticed a figure in a bright yellow Bromley shirt across the bar. It was Ian. I suspected he'd already had a similar conversation.

The Bromley players and management turned up not long after, and the evening soon turned into the perfect illustration of what makes non-league football so special. The manager, Neil Smith, was buying drinks for all the fans who had made the trip (although he looked unimpressed when I asked for a glass of water). The players and everyone else from the club were mixing freely, playing pool (Brandon Hanlan and Louis Dennis were the standouts, with Hanlan eventually winning an epic battle against his fellow striker) and darts (central defenders Jack Holland, Roger Johnson and Ben Chorley were the pick) with supporters.

I enjoyed getting to talk to some of them – Smith was likeable, open and honest; George Porter, who could be a bit niggly on the field, couldn't have been nicer off it; and Jerry Dolke wasn't just the owner, he also came across as being a passionate fan of the club.

Meanwhile, right back Luke Woolfenden, who looked as though he'd never drunk alcohol before, was being introduced to the delights of Dark Fruit, the cider of choice for many of the travelling fans. Some of them, including Lloyd and Pete, were so fond of it that they went by the name of the 'Dark Fruit Ultras'.

By the time we left, around nine, the whole last-minute postponement thing seemed to have been forgotten and everyone was having a great time. The general feeling was that there was no chance of the pitch being ready for the following week and that it might make sense to find somewhere else to play the game.

That didn't stop Spennymoor insisting that it would take place at their ground the following Tuesday night. As the week went by, there were encouraging sounds from Brewery Field. They were confident that the pitch would be ready but the BBC weather app showed that rain was forecast from Saturday onwards. Would there be another wasted journey?

Spennymoor then made an announcement on Twitter. If the game was called off on Tuesday, it would take place on Wednesday. By this stage I was so confused that I had no idea which train to book, if any.

Things were further complicated by announcements that there would be a pitch inspection on Monday and, if it failed, the game would instead be played at nearby Darlington's ground on Wednesday. A Spennymoor fan, who seemed to have inside knowledge, came on the Bromley forum and said that the weather was fine, the problem area of the pitch was covered and he was confident that the game would take place at Brewery Field on Tuesday. A few minutes after that appeared, the FA announced that it would take place at the rather grandly named Northern Echo Arena in Darlington on Wednesday.

I arranged to travel up with Pete and we got the train to Darlington. During the journey, he expressed the strong opinion that the game should have been played at Durham Women's ground in Belmont, which had an artificial surface and was just down the road from Spennymoor. I have no idea how Pete knows things like this. He also seems to know the exact location of Wetherspoon's in every town in the country, and suggested we head to one of Darlington's two Wether-spoon's, The William Stead (named after a former editor of the *Northern Echo* who was one of the passengers who died on the *Titanic*), for a prematch meal.

I thought this was a brilliant idea for several reasons, the prime one being that I'd never actually been to a Spoons (as aficionados call them) before. All I knew about them was that football fans always met at the nearest one to whatever ground they were visiting, that the founder of the pub chain looked like something out of a Wurzels tribute band and that there were people travelling up and down the country trying to visit all 900-odd Wetherspoon's branches, hoping to get a pictorial about themselves in the quarterly magazine known to regulars as *Spoons News*.

More importantly, I'd be able to get chips and there was a very real chance I'd be called 'pet'.

Although I would be disappointed on the 'pet' front, the chips more than made up for it and we got to the ground with around half an hour to spare. I wasn't sure whether we were meant to use the HOME or AWAY supporters' entrance until one of Pete's mates pointed out that it didn't matter, as both teams were away.

The first thing I did on entering the ground was to lean over the hoardings and take a close look at the state of the pitch. Although there had been reassurances that there was no doubt about the game going ahead, I was still nervous.

At least there was one benefit from all the postponements – because of the delay, we knew who the winners of the match would be playing in the semi-final. It wasn't Brackley from the level below us, who we were hoping to get. It would be Gateshead, a far tougher proposition.

It was a wild, windy night and about thirty Bromley fans had made the journey, most of them on a coach that had been paid for by a collection of local businesses, including a window installer, an accountancy firm and an air-conditioning company. Ian had driven up again, this time with Tim and Uncle Gary. Like me, he would have been disappointed to see that the Darlington club shop was closed but, to be honest, that saved us having to deal with a controversial issue.

It was a grey area in the developing world of competitive non-league mug collecting – does it count if you get a mug from Darlington, a team that play at the ground you're at, even if it's not that team you're playing?

And that wasn't the only thing occupying my mind as the game kicked off. I was still trying to work out what the sign behind us in the stand meant ('OUR FOOTBALL CLUBS ARE FOR NOT JUST FOR BUSINESS'), when Spennymoor took the lead, as Glen Taylor turned on the edge of the box and beat David Gregory at the near post with a perfectly struck drive. A familiar air of gloom settled over the contingent of Bromley fans. We were 1-0 down and playing a side with a goalkeeper incapable of conceding against Bromley.

The depression was worse than I had ever experienced

watching my team. It suddenly became clear that, the further you go in an FA Cup or Trophy run, the tougher it gets.

Then, a minute or two after conceding the goal, Frankie Raymond played a through ball but slightly overhit it and Lowson came out to clear the danger. And that was when the goalkeeper, whom I'd built up to be some kind of cross between Gordon Banks and David de Gea, took a comedy air-swing at the ball with his right foot, missing it by a considerable distance and it bounced past him. Louis Dennis, barely able to believe his luck, jogged past him and tucked the ball into an empty net. Bromley were level.

As the game settled into a pattern of half chances to both sides, I noticed Lloyd had struck up a conversation with half a dozen young Darlington fans, who looked to be around fourteen or fifteen years of age. They were telling Lloyd that they'd come along to support Bromley against their hated local rivals. They had all enjoyed the equalising goal, especially a smallish ginger-haired boy with glasses.

After that, both sides went close, with Louis Dennis having done all the hard work by beating about a million defenders before hitting a weak shot straight at Lowson. At the other end, David Gregory tipped the ball round the post.

It was then that I became aware of Joe Tait, the big Spennymoor centre back, who had come up for the corner, screaming something in our direction. I couldn't quite make out what he was saying, but the gist seemed to be that he wanted to fight us afterwards. All of us.

According to Lloyd, it wasn't us but the group of boys he was shouting at. I'd missed it, but apparently they'd been winding him up all game. At half-time, Tait was still screaming abuse as he left the field.

For the second half, we switched ends, which meant the cold wind was blowing directly into our faces, but we were rewarded ten minutes after the break. Frankie Raymond swung a free kick into the crowded penalty area, which was missed by everyone (including Joe Tait). Jack Holland timed his run well to meet the ball, but it was unclear whether he had got a touch to it or it had gone directly into the net. The Bromley players and fans didn't care – the previously unbeatable Lowson had been beaten again and we were 2-1 up.

One man who wasn't sharing the happiness was Tait. He was shouting at everyone from his teammates to the young Darlington fans who, it was clear, were increasingly getting to him. The more he reacted, the funnier they seemed to find it. Things got even worse when Tait missed a golden chance to equalise, hitting the ball straight at Gregory from a yard out. The Darlington boys let him know that he should have scored, the ginger one shouting 'You've cost your team a day out at Wembley!'

And that was the nearest the game came to another goal. Louis Dennis and Brandon Hanlan both had good chances but couldn't finish them. It had been a messy game in truth, played in blustery conditions.

The final whistle led to wild scenes of celebration from the Bromley and Darlington fans. It was a hugely important win and I have rarely felt such excitement after a game. I knew that sleep would be hard to come by that night.

As the players trooped off through a tunnel of yellow-vested security guards, Tait's tormentors hadn't finished.

'What was the score, Tait?' said one, as the centre back walked past. 'Well played Taity,' said another. 'Well played Joe Tait,' said the ginger, laughing and applauding him.

And that was when Joe Tait snapped. He pointed to the ginger kid in glasses and did the sort of impression a five-year-old would have been delighted with – he made circles with his thumbs and forefingers and held them up to his eyes. 'Speccy virgin!' he screamed at the young man, as he made his way towards him. 'You're a speccy virgin!'

That was when a small group of Spennymoor girls, who looked to be around thirteen years old, decided to get involved. 'See you at school tomorrow!' shouted one, menacingly, in the direction of the young ginger. But he was enjoying himself too much to care. Eventually, Tait was dragged into the changing room by a couple of teammates, some of whom had joined in the 'speccy' insults and had copied the glasses gesture. The ginger kid looked happier than he'd probably ever been in his life.

I glanced back beyond the departing players to the sign on the terraces. 'OUR FOOTBALL CLUBS ARE FOR NOT JUST FOR BUSINESS'. It still made no sense.

As I made my way out of the ground, I found myself alongside Georgie, the youngest of the Weavers, who had a look of stunned disbelief on her face. 'We're in the FA Trophy semifinal,' she said. I nodded, but it hadn't really sunk in with either of us.

It was hard to believe. But that weekend, we'd play Gateshead at Hayes Lane in the first leg of the FA Trophy semi-final.

And I wouldn't be there.

CHAPTER SIXTEEN

It was an incredibly painful decision, but it had to be made. I just couldn't afford to go to the first leg of the semi-final as well as the second, so I had opted to miss out on the trip to Hayes Lane.

The game was taking place just three days after beating Spennymoor at Darlington, which was probably how long it would take Joe Tait to calm down.

When Saturday came around, I realised I would be unable to calmly sit down and listen to the game. Instead, I walked around the streets of Guiseley with my headphones on to listen to the BBC commentary from Hayes Lane. I was still adjusting them when Gateshead took the lead with less than a minute gone. A cruel, deflected goal. Perhaps it just wasn't meant to be. The commentator reckoned that Gateshead could have been 3-0 up after about fifteen minutes, had a couple of attempts gone in and not hit the post.

But as I was walking past Tony Woods Quality Butchers ('Home of the famous Guiseley Growler sausage'), Bromley were awarded a penalty following a foul on Brandon Hanlan. It sounded a bit of a soft one, but Hanlan scored from the spot and the scores were level. I have rarely felt such a sense of relief.

Just before half-time, as I was about to reach North Hair Design, Gateshead took the lead again. And any remaining hope drained out of me. I had always thought that when people said that something felt like a dagger through the heart that they were exaggerating. That was when I discovered they weren't. That was exactly how it felt.

I had a mini-tantrum and ripped the headphones off, put them in my pocket and tried to clear any thoughts of football from my mind.

It didn't work, but I was scared to check the result when I got home, afraid of what I might see. If the commentary was anything to go by, it might have been an embarrassingly heavy loss.

While I was considering whether it would be best to just know the score, rather than worry about it all night, T. J. Herbert, the *Bromley Boys* film producer, rang.

'You'll be a happy man,' he said. What was he talking about? I was crushed and demoralised. 'Good result for you.'

'What, Bromley? Why, what was the score?' I said, hope rising inside me. 'I had to stop listening after we went 2-1 down.'

'You won 3-2.'

It turned out that Louis Dennis (who else?) had scored twice in the second half and I felt a glimmer of hope where there had previously been none.

And then the day got even better. The reason he'd rung was to tell me that I'd definitely be going to Wembley regardless of what happened in the second leg of the FA Trophy semi-final at Gateshead next Saturday – he'd booked the stadium for the premiere of *The Bromley Boys*.

It was going to be a huge occasion with a star-studded red carpet, although I hadn't actually heard of any of the stars. They were from reality shows, which was apparently a tactic designed to make sure press photographers turned up.

But far more exciting, for me anyway, was the news that Alan Stonebridge and Alan Soper, my heroes from the 1969/70 team, had been invited and had accepted, as had Neil Smith and Jack Holland, the present-day Bromley manager and captain respectively.

Once T. J. and I had finished our conversation, I went onto Twitter to find out if away goals counted double. If they did, we were in trouble, having conceded twice at home in the first leg. I was hugely relieved when I found out that they didn't. Bromley had gone from no chance to having an outside chance. A draw at Gateshead would be enough. Even a 1–0 loss would mean extra time.

My mood had been completely transformed. Hope can do that to you. The next seven days passed in a blur. Disturbed sleep started around Wednesday night and by Saturday morning I was wide awake by five.

I had decided to travel to Gateshead on my own, as I wasn't sure I'd be able to carry out a coherent conversation with anyone. I had booked a train that would get me to Newcastle three hours before kick-off. That way, even if the train, as well as the next three, were cancelled, I'd still arrive in enough time. I didn't want to leave anything to chance.

Gazing out of the window, multiple scenarios played out in my head, from worst case (I'd started worrying about a 9–0 humiliation – apparently I hadn't got over Sutton beating us by that scoreline in 1968) to best case (a glorious draw). Not once did I consider a Bromley win.

I watched nervously as we crossed the bridge high over the River Tyne and pulled into the station at a few seconds after 1.16 p.m. I knew this because I'd downloaded a stopwatch app for the match, so I'd know exactly how long was left. I knew from a previous visit to Gateshead that the stadium didn't have a clock.

I walked the streets of Newcastle for twenty-eight minutes

and fifteen seconds, trying to get rid of some of the tension, and then found a café near the station. I wasn't hungry but, for the sake of the team, I asked for a plate of chips.

'Chips? That all you want, pet?' said the woman behind the counter.

It took a second to sink in. Finally, on my fourth trip of the season to the north-east, someone had called me 'pet'. Perhaps this was a sign, although that would be pushing it.

I was still too nervous to have an appetite but, for perhaps the only time in my life, I forced myself to polish off the chips. I didn't want to blame myself if we lost.

I then got on the Metro, which was just across the road, and made my way to the ambitiously named International Stadium. Having been designed for athletics, it wasn't a great place to watch football, with the running track surrounding the pitch meaning the action was a fair distance from the stand. There was usually a complete lack of atmosphere but, as soon as I caught sight of the ground, I knew today would be different.

There were queues stretching for hundreds and hundreds of yards and what seemed like thousands of people milling around. It probably helped that none of Newcastle, Sunderland or Middlesbrough were playing at home, but this was going to be quite a crowd.

I got a couple of programmes, which I had to queue for. I flicked through one of them and saw that the penalty last week was a sore point as far as Gateshead were concerned. The gaffer, Steve Watson, used his column 'The Gaffer' to call it 'a huge error'; skipper Neill Byrne in his 'Captain's Column' called it 'particularly disappointing'; while press officer Dominic Scurr used his 'Press Pack' piece to say 'the less said about that penalty the better'.

At least I didn't have to bother with the extra stress of buying a mug and transporting it home without breaking it. I'd already got one on my last visit earlier in the season. It showed the Angel of the

North with a gigantic football at his/her feet, and sat proudly on my shelf, between Fylde and Guiseley.

But my collection was nowhere near as impressive as Ian's, and he'd managed to stretch his lead in recent weeks. I'd briefly considered an idea to make up ground on him by getting mugs via mail order, but I felt that this would be cheating and that the world of competitive non-league mug collecting could ill afford the scandal.

It was a shame because there were several mugs I had my eyes on, having spent many an hour visiting the websites of non-league clubs' shops and looking at their mugs from a collector's point of view.

The Fakenham Town one, which showed what looked like a ghost carrying a large rolling pin on its shoulders, felt like a 'must have', while Scarborough Athletic's mug had a picture of a psychotic seagull, sitting above the words 'No Battle, No Victory'. All seagulls are scary, but this one was genuinely terrifying.

Another mug I had my eye on was from Leamington FC, which showed a windmill about to be knocked down by a giant football (which looked remarkably similar to the one at the foot of the Angel of the North).

But mugs were soon replaced by the FA Trophy in my thoughts as I made my way through the turnstile and into the ground. The first thing I noticed was that there was a huge turnout of Bromley fans, and most appeared to be as nervous as I was. I looked around and found plenty of familiar faces.

Garvo was there, a man so committed to the club that when he injured his leg on the way to a game against Ashford Town (in Middlesex) he insisted on being wheeled from the station to the ground in a rickety old shopping trolley, which had a wheel missing.

Sue, who was standing next to him, had been going to Hayes Lane since she was a baby (her mum worked in the tea hut) and hardly missed a game. She often lay down on the luggage rack in trains which, somehow, was a demonstration of how much she hated Sutton.

David Gregory (Senior), who had arrived by train several hours before me, was the one I felt for most. I'd seen how much he suffered in games that didn't really matter. Watching his son in such an important game – one mistake could mean his team missing out on a trip to Wembley – was going to be tougher than usual.

He was with Half-Time John (whose name came from arriving at half-time for home games, after picking up his daughter Ellie) and the Weavers, whom he'd met up with in the local Spoons (The Tilley Stone, a name derived from Gateshead's coal-mining past – I was starting to discover that the pubs provided a rich seam of local history). It seemed that every Bromley fan I'd ever encountered had made the trip, and everyone I spoke to said that they hadn't slept well. Many, like me, had given up on getting any sleep long before dawn.

Only one person seemed relaxed and he was the least likely of all to be in that state. Mash, who I had never seen even remotely confident about Bromley's prospects, didn't appear to have a worry in the world. He even seemed surprised that I looked stressed.

'We'll win,' he said. 'No problem. Don't know what you're worried about.'

I wasn't convinced. This was so out of character that I suspected it was his way of coping with the enormity of what was about to take place. Mash had once said that, when watching Bromley during some of their darkest times, he had seen things no man should ever see. I thought he, of all people, understood the futility of hope.

Col, the fanzine editor, who I stood alongside, was more

consistent. 'Can't see us winning,' he said, echoing my thoughts.

The Bromley end was filling up and I caught sight of Roy and his disco-dancing brother. I went over to talk to Roy and he was as excited as I'd seen him since we had taken the lead against West Ham in a preseason friendly in 1969.

I think everyone just wanted the game to start. But as kick-off time approached, there was no sign of the players. What was going on? An announcement over the tannoy soon cleared things up. There was going to be a delay of ten minutes because people were still trying to get into the ground. This was not a problem Bromley fans were familiar with, but it confirmed what a big match this was.

The sprinklers were still on when the teams finally walked out of the tunnel, which was surprising given the amount of rain that had fallen recently just down the road at Spennymoor. Was this some kind of bizarre attempt to get the game postponed?

I wanted to see if the Bromley players looked confident or nervous but, since the tunnel was about two miles from where we were standing, it was impossible.

It didn't take long for everyone to leave the comfort of their seats and stand up. When the referee got the game underway, I set my new stopwatch app, which would tell me exactly how much time was left in the half, down to one-hundredth of a second.

There were still forty-four minutes and fifteen seconds left when I first checked. This was going to be agony. Every time the ball was in the Bromley half, I felt overcome with nerves. How could anyone enjoy watching football?

There were only five minutes and a few seconds gone when Louis Dennis found Brandon Hanlan inside the area. His shot was parried away by James Montgomery in the Gateshead goal, but the ball hit defender Fraser Kerr, who was rushing back to help his keeper (whose grandfather, I would have gleaned if I hadn't been too nervous to discover this at the time, was the cousin of legendary 1973 Sunderland FA Cup-winning keeper Jim Montgomery).

Watching the ball slowly loop into the unguarded net from the full-back's knee was one of the most beautiful sights I had ever seen. My heart felt as though it was about to burst. Of all the various doom-laden scenarios I had conjured up, none of them included a Bromley goal. The feeling of euphoria swept across the stand, many unable to believe what they'd just seen.

When Frankie Raymond came close to adding a second, a fleeting thought crossed my mind. Had Mash been right all along? Was it possible we could win? I dismissed it immediately. It was far too soon. But our defence seemed to have the measure of the Gateshead attack. Luke Woolfenden looked to have suffered no long-term effect from his Dark Fruit baptism and was having one of his best games, while Jordan Higgs was superb. Jack Holland and Roger Johnson were winning pretty much everything in the air.

In the second half, in truth, not much seemed to be happening, with chances for both sides restricted to a handful of long-range efforts. But then Gateshead started to look more threatening and, after coming close with a couple of attempts which were blocked, came a moment that made me feel physically sick.

With twenty-one minutes and thirty-two seconds left, a clearance bounced out to Scott Barrow, who was at least thirty-five yards out. What happened next took place directly in front of us. Barrow lined up a shot and I have rarely seen a ball struck so sweetly. It seemed to be flying towards the top right-hand corner in slow motion; David Gregory launched himself towards where it was heading, but no goalkeeper on earth could have stopped it.

It was 1-1 and another goal from Gateshead, which felt inevitable, would mean extra time. The home side would have the momentum and finish Bromley off, probably by a score of 3-1. Maybe even 4-1, from a controversial penalty to even things up after last week. I'd come up with this entire scenario within seconds of Barrow's goal.

But we were holding out and, as the tension became almost unbearable, I looked over at Mash. He'd been unusually quiet throughout the match (he could normally be relied upon to issue single-word instructions to the players such as 'inflict', 'induce' or 'instigate' in a Dalek-like monotone) and was now swaying unsteadily on his feet. I asked him if he was OK; he just said that he was feeling a bit faint and needed to sit down, which he did. All pretence of casual indifference was gone.

I was staring at my stopwatch app constantly, watching every second tick by. Time seemed to have virtually come to a standstill and the last ten minutes seemed to last at least ten hours. Every time Gateshead got the ball, a goal felt certain. But with Gateshead pushing forward, Bromley were looking more likely to score on the break and Louis Dennis and Josh Rees both had chances.

And then, as the ball went out for a goal kick to Bromley, Ben Tower (Blackburn) blew the whistle. The Gateshead players crumpled to the turf. There was a split second of stunned silence while it all sank in and then the hugging, dancing and jumping up and down began.

I found myself hugging Col, saying, 'We did it. We did it.' Will, a fellow Northern exile and a regular at away games, clenched his fist and ran around in a small circle shouting 'Yeeees!' Mash, expressionless, held his black, white and red scarf above his head. Ian, in his white Bromley shirt, was almost delirious. You could see how much it meant to everyone.

I then sank to my seat, head in hands, hoping no one would see the tears that were running down my face. I needn't have worried. As I looked around, I saw that I wasn't the only one. Faces which just seconds ago had shown signs of unbearable tension were now lit up with happiness and pride, with tears of joy and relief.

David Gregory (Senior) rushed down the steps to the front as David Gregory (Junior) leaped over the barriers separating the players from the fans and headed for his dad. They embraced each other for almost a minute, seemingly oblivious to all the noise and chaos around them. Some of the other Bromley players pushed aside the barriers and made their way to the front, where they were engulfed. The rest soon joined them, as did the manager, coaching staff and Jerry Dolke and his wife Julia. Neil Smith had leapt into the crowd while George Porter was doing a dance that was unlikely to lead to an invitation to appear on *Strictly*.

Lloyd and the fans around him were proudly holding a huge Bromley flag above their heads. The Weavers seemed to be hugging everyone within a ten-yard radius. Supporters – and players – were standing, applauding and singing the same song over and over again. 'We're the famous Brom-er-lee and we're off to Wember-lee.' It was one of the most memorable moments in fifty years of watching Bromley and I just wanted the feeling to last forever.

But I had a train to catch, so reluctantly tore myself away. I walked down the hill with Roy, who hadn't stopped smiling since the final whistle, quietly allowing it to sink in. Roy was still beaming as he got on the coach and I made my way to the station. On the train back, I read the match report on the Gateshead website. Their manager, Steve Watson, said that 'the key moments were the penalty that wasn't in the first game and then gifting them the opening goal today.'

By the time I got home, someone had posted a video of fans, including Garvo, Sue, Mash and Ian, on the train – and Tube – back to Bromley. They were singing 'We're the famous Bromer-lee and we're off to Wem-ber-lee' over and over again. Random passengers were joining in.

The words 'We're off to Wem-ber-lee' finally sank in.

It was the thing I'd wanted most when I had started watching Bromley over fifty years earlier. We had finally banished the ghosts of the 1949 team.

CHAPTER SEVENTEEN

Who would we play in the final? Wealdstone or Brackley? I was hoping it would be Wealdstone, a club responsible for a lot of good memories. But it wasn't to be; we would be meeting Brackley Town – from the Conference North – in the FA Trophy final.

But it didn't really matter who the opposition were. Because, after waiting for fifty long years, I was going to watch Bromley play at Wembley.

The night before the final, I put my tickets on the dining table to make sure I didn't forget to take them. There were four of them in total – two for Liz and two for me. We each had a ticket to sit with the Bromley fans behind one of the goals and a ticket to sit in a corporate box.

We'd been invited by Alan Alger, a fairly high-profile non-league fan who had a small part in the *Bromley Boys* film as a reporter. The day before the game, he'd emailed to say that he and I were going to be doing a short interview on TV as part of the build-up. The thought was terrifying, but I could hardly say no.

On the morning of the game, I was still unsure which tickets we'd be using. Should I sit amongst the people I'd stood alongside throughout the run to the final? Or should I go against every principle I'd ever held and sit in a box that was symptomatic of the corporate greed that had blighted football?

I was leaning toward the latter.

The Wembley website had a superb way to help us make a final decision – an 'interactive tool' which showed the view from every seat in the stadium – and I decided to compare the two. The view from the box was directly behind the goal, while the seat was closer to the pitch, but halfway between the goal and the corner flag.

Five hours later, we were walking down Wembley Way, on the way to our corporate box. The weather was gorgeous, with the sun beaming down. It was a unique experience going to a Bromley FA Trophy game that wasn't in the depths of winter, a sign of how unsuccessful we'd been in the past.

I had no choice but to spend a fiver on a small box of chips, which were so ordinary that I threw them away before finishing them. I just hoped that I'd eaten enough to avoid jinxing Bromley.

There were also people selling half-and-half scarves, rosettes and flags, but I wasn't tempted. I already had my souvenir sorted – a special limited-edition mug, which had been organised by Sue and Simon. And at £5 it was literally as cheap as chips.

As we walked towards the stadium, my heart was beating rapidly. This was what I'd been waiting for and, as it sunk in that this was really happening, I found myself looking back once again at the long road I'd taken to finally get to Wembley.

I thought of the framed black and white photo from 1949, now presumed lost in The Great Fire of 1992, which had started the dream. I could still see it now – Eric Fright being held aloft by his Bromley teammates as he proudly clutched the Amateur Cup, while George Brown stared with joyous disbelief at his medal, against a backdrop of tens of thousands of cheering fans.

I remembered the time when my hopes of glory had been cruelly smashed by Sutton when they had beaten us 9–0 at an age when I was barely able to cope with such humiliation. And my mind wandered back to those never-ending trips to countless games against Folkestone and Shepway, where the sides eventually got so fed up with each other that they ended up having an on-field battle.

There were other random memories. My scooter, which had taken me to a Trophy tie, and my three-wheeler, which had never had the chance. And the time Bromley scraped the depths by losing to the Diddymen, which was made even worse by sitting in front of the most annoying fans in the whole of football.

And then there was Jack Holland's late goal against Workington. Without that, we wouldn't have been here today.

The nearer we got to the stadium, the more excited I became. The crowd milling around outside was already far bigger than I'd ever seen at a Bromley game and I'd already met four or five people I knew – a tiny part of the 14,000-strong contingent currently making their way there.

This would include several fans flying vast distances into the UK and then flying home straight afterwards. Steve had left New Zealand on Wednesday, Nick from San Francisco had arrived a week ago and Andrew had left on Thursday from the Gold Coast of Australia. All for a game of non-league football.

Nearer to home, David Gregory (Senior) was bringing 256 friends and family from all around the country, putting on two coaches and two double-decker buses. Another coachload of his friends was coming directly from Liverpool.

There was a queue to get into the stadium as security was tight. Once we got in, after being thoroughly searched, we had to take four escalators, which was another first for a Bromley game.

The last time I'd been to Wembley was on a wet night in 1981, when I'd seen England play Hungary with my friend Kevin. At the time I had to put both of my programmes into a carrier bag to avoid them getting a soaking. That was why I was especially happy to see an exciting new innovation to delight programme collectors everywhere – programmes at Wembley came in a small, specially designed, programme-sized plastic bag.

I bought four of them (which used up my food budget of £20), although I was sorely tempted to take them back as soon as I opened the very first page, which was headed BROMLEY TOWN. Why do people call us Bromley Town? There is no such team. Bromley Town is the name of a bowling club, not a football club.

The rest of the programme was better. It was great to see an interview with Club Shop Jim (formerly Club Canteen Assistant Jim), who had started watching Bromley long before I did. It was also interesting to read Jack Holland's comments on the Bromley players ('George Porter will come in the changing room and just start dancing').

I also learned a bit about our opponents from their captain Gareth Dean, and was especially looking forward to seeing Ellis Myles ('He thinks he's some kind of model but he's got a terrible haircut') and Matt Lowe ('Runs like a three-legged camel').

But there was only time for a brief read, as Alan and I had to find our way to the BT interview, past about a dozen layers of security, yellow-vested men with walkie-talkies closely checking our lanyards.

Eventually we were herded into a tiny area just yards from where the tunnel met the pitch. And that was where I came face to face with someone I'd last seen on TV reporting from Hartley Wintney against Bromley back in the first round. I'd also seen him the previous day on the front of a postcode lottery mailer, in which he had been standing holding a clipboard under the headline '£11 MILLION WILL BE WON IN JUNE!'

We all introduced ourselves and it turned out the reporter's name was Jeff. After talking briefly about the game, which was now less than an hour away, Alan and I stood there against a backdrop of 'BUILDBASE. BUILDING AND TIMBER SUPPLIES' logos, waiting for Jeff to get the signal to start. He then got the nod and we were underway.

I was feeling quite important – a feeling that vanished when Jeff got two words into the interview.

'So, Alan,' he said to me, 'you've written a book about…'

'Er, I'm Dave,' I said and, indicating the man on my right, 'he's Alan.'

'Sorry about that,' Jeff said, turning to the cameraman. 'Let's do that again.'

'So, Dave,' he said. 'You've written a book about the Bromley Boys and it's about to be adapted into a screenplay.'

'Yeah, comes out on Thursday right here at Wembley,' I replied and then, realising that this was a bit of a short answer, added, 'Looking forward to it.'

He only asked me one more question after that, wanting to know why I had written the book in the first place. I babbled something that made little sense and he quickly switched his attention to Alan.

A minute later it was over. I wandered towards the pitch, to see if I could get a glimpse of it before going up to the box we'd be watching the game from. I kept looking around for security guards, but none stopped me. I kept walking, out of the tunnel and into the bright May sunshine, imagining what it was going to be like for the Bromley players. The stadium looked vast and the playing surface, which was being watered, perfect – especially considering the FA Cup final had taken place there just twenty-four hours earlier.

I decided to push my luck and see if I could get away with going for a walk around the pitch. I spotted a few dozen Bromley fans who had taken their seats early, soaking up the atmosphere. They must have wondered what I was doing.

I saw Col, who didn't look as though he could quite believe he was at Wembley to watch Bromley, and we had a chat about how bizarre it felt being there. In the next section, Joe, who was around twelve or thirteen, was sitting near the front. I was a bit worried that he'd think playing at Wembley was normal, but he seemed sensible enough and I'd seen him at enough terrible games over the years to think he'd probably be OK.

Then my phone rang. It was Liz.

'What are you doing on the pitch?' she asked, accusingly, having spotted me from the box. Busted by my own wife. I said that I'd be with her shortly.

As I walked back towards the tunnel, imagining the crowd chanting my name after my spectacular last-minute winner had won Bromley the Trophy, the real Bromley players were coming out. They didn't look particularly nervous, although a few were just looking around, taking it all in.

I had a quick word with a couple of those that I'd spoken to at the pub in Spennymoor and then made my way to the luxury of the executive box. Once there, I got talking to Alan's dad, Gerry, a Hayes Lane regular and season-ticket holder for the past twelve years, and his wife Lindsay. They were as nervous as I was and it didn't help when Alan, who worked for Betway, told us that Bromley were strong favourites.

Even though Alan had laid on quite a spread, I didn't have anything to eat. The half box of chips had been enough. There was a row of seats in front of the box, where we sat down and soaked up the atmosphere. The view was spectacular, exactly as it looked on the website.

I looked out at the scene in front of me and it felt as though I was experiencing a perfect day. The sun was beaming down as Jack Holland led the Bromley team out onto the Wembley pitch, with Louis Dennis, fresh from being named in the National League team of the year, applauding the fans. There was a party atmosphere.

Somewhere amongst the vast sea of Bromley fans directly in front of us were the twenty or thirty people you'd see at every Bromley away game, whether it was on a Saturday at Sutton or a Tuesday night in Torquay.

There were also loads of new faces, including the dozen twentysomethings a couple of rows from us, who were arguing amongst themselves about whether Bromley were the team in white shirts or the team in red and white stripes.

The sense of pride I was feeling was immense, especially when Jack introduced the team to the dignitaries. I couldn't make out who they were, but the previous day, in the FA Cup final, Prince William had been the guest of honour. It turned out that the FA Trophy had a man with a slightly lower profile – the Buildbase Procurement Director.

And then everyone stood for the national anthem, which I normally mumbled along to self-consciously. This time, I joined in loudly and with feeling, getting completely caught up in the moment.

David Gregory (Junior) ran towards us, with a wave. This was perfect – I liked to be behind the goal we were attacking in the second half.

The game finally got underway. A game I had waited fifty years to see. It was end-to-end action in the opening minutes. A long ball virtually straight from the kick-off almost put Omar Bugiel through and, at the other end, Matt Lowe (whose day job was building prototype cars as part of Jaguar Land Rover's design team) had a half chance.

But then, after twenty minutes, Adam Mekki went off on one of his mazy runs, held off the defender and played a ball through to Omar Bugiel. The Lebanese international (no, really) took a touch and rifled the ball past the diving Danny Lewis (an interior designer and fitter for show homes) into the bottom corner and Bromley were ahead. At first, we were unsure that it had really happened since the sound from the far end of the vast stadium took a second or so to reach us.

But when it did, and it was confirmed that we were in the lead, I was overcome with sheer joy. I've felt excitement before, but never at this level. Bromley had just scored at the same end as Geoff Hurst, when he netted his 'They think it's all over' goal in 1966 (despite minor details like this being a completely new pitch in a completely rebuilt stadium). Liz greeted this historical fact-sharing by announcing that she was going to get herself another glass of wine.

And she wasn't the only one with a thirst. The heat was such that there was an official break midway through the half for the players to have a drink (I'd noticed Adam Mekki calling for a water bottle after only ten minutes).

Ten minutes later, George Porter nearly made it two, but his volley from just inside the area was well saved by Lewis. But whatever was happening on the pitch, the Bromley fans had never stopped singing and they never did. Even though the rest of the half produced little to get excited about.

It was a relief to get to the break with our 1-0 lead intact. 1-0, just as in Bromley's 1949 FA Amateur Cup win at Wembley. 1-0, just as in Bromley's two other victories in the competition, in 1938 and 1911. We were halfway to winning the FA Trophy. Halfway to making history.

During the break, Liz and I went to meet Kevin, the friend with whom I'd been to Wembley all those years ago. We had a drink, talked and took some photos of us posing by the Three Lions statues and at the back of the Bobby Moore statue, which I immediately posted on Instagram.

Meanwhile, out on the pitch, a freestyle footballer with literally millions of YouTube followers was showing some impressive tricks. As half-time entertainment went, this was a step up from cheerleaders and Minnie Mouse and, by the time we'd got back to the box, the teams were already out on the pitch.

I was feeling a bit better about life after the break. We'd probably just shaded the first half, but I was pretty sure Brackley fans would have felt that they had.

My growing confidence went into sharp reverse when Shane Byrne (labourer and dressing-room DJ) shot just wide. It was a reminder that the game wasn't over yet. This was followed by a flurry of further reminders which came in four second-half minutes in which Brackley could – and should – have scored four times.

Aaron Williams tried to turn in a cross, but his shot was cleared off the line by Roger Johnson. James Armson hit the post from only a few yards out. Williams then had a shot smartly saved by Gregory but looked certain to score from the rebound, until Jordan Higgs made a brilliant goal-line clearance. The Brackley manager, Kevin Wilkin, then planted his face in his hands for the fourth time in as many minutes when Armson sliced wide when it would have been easier to score.

Throughout all this, the Bromley fans never stopped singing. They sang about going down the Masons Hill to see the Bromley aces, they sang about how much they loved Bromley and they sang about going to Wem-ber-lee.

Not long after the series of near misses, Bromley switched to a more defensive formation which seemed to have the desired effect. With around twenty minutes left on the clock there was the first sign of the game drawing to a close, when a swarm of orange-vested stewards appeared from nowhere and took their places in front of the stands and behind the goals.

Bromley were in full parking-the-bus-and-running-the-clock-down mode, but still looked threatening on the break. Just a minute from time, Brandon Hanlan was given the chance to ensure his place in history by adding a second. Josh Rees, who had made a difference since coming on, played a lovely ball through to the Charlton loanee, leaving him with just Lewis to beat.

In front of Bromley fans roaring encouragement, his shot

went straight at the keeper's legs and 14,000 hearts sank. Still, there wasn't long to go, just a few minutes of injury time.

Then the fourth official held up a board that produced a gasp of disbelief from the Bromley fans in front of us. He was indicating five minutes of added time. FIVE MINUTES. How was I meant to cope with that?

I started the stopwatch app on my phone. I hadn't needed it during the ninety minutes because there was a clock on the giant screen.

In the first minute of added time, the ball stayed mainly in the Brackley half. Frankie Sutherland took the ball into the corner and kept it there to waste a few precious seconds.

With less than four minutes to go, Armson broke through the Bromley defence, only for David Gregory to make an incredible save. The resulting corner was dealt with by Roger Johnson.

With less than three minutes to go, the Brackley keeper came up for yet another corner. He collided with Gregory and they both fell to the ground. It was a bizarre sight, two goalkeepers lying next to each other. Soon after, Jack Holland made a great block when the Brackley striker once again looked likely to score.

With less than two minutes to go, there was yet another corner, which Gregory – who was my Man of the Match – caught and then fell to the ground, clutching the ball. My nerves were shredded. I seriously thought about just closing my eyes so I didn't have to go through it. The whistles from the Bromley fans were deafening. I even tried joining in, but have never been able to whistle properly.

With less than a minute to go, the ball was loose in the Bromley penalty area and the strain was unbearable – until Roger Johnson reacted first and walloped it into the stand. This was a good tactic, since there was only one ball. This was not a sign of the FA economising, but because fetching it back gave small breaks in play so that players could take a drink in the searing heat.

That was when I tentatively felt the tiniest rays of hope. Surely we were safe now? I looked at my stopwatch app for what seemed like the thousandth time. In just thirty seconds, Chris Kavanagh (Manchester) would blow his whistle and the celebrations would begin.

Then Jack Holland would lead his team up the 107 steps to receive the Trophy, before lifting it to the delight of more than ten thousand cheering, singing Bromley fans.

I could barely believe I was there to see it.

EPILOGUE

The next time I watched Bromley was three months later, at home to Gateshead. We won with a controversial goal from Junior Ogedi-Uzokwe, a few minutes from time, giving us our first win of the season after five games.

The controversial goal wasn't really controversial. I was right behind the goal and it definitely crossed the line. But I would say that, wouldn't I?

Although I loved watching Bromley again, I still hadn't got over seeing us concede a goal against Brackley with twenty-one seconds left on the clock in the FA Trophy final, and doubted I ever would. Liz told me that I'd sunk to my knees screaming 'Noooooooooooo!', as the unlucky Roger Johnson poked the ball into his own net, following some penalty-box pinball.

I also hadn't even begun to recover from losing on penalties, after we'd taken a 3-1 lead and just needed the next spot kick to go in for the Trophy to be ours. It didn't.

The other thing I was unlikely to ever get over was the sight of the Brackley players celebrating their victory as Liz and I dashed to the stadium exit, having failed to allow for extra time when booking our advance train tickets. We missed our train and had to pay a small fortune to get back to Leeds.

It hadn't been a good day.

I hadn't managed to watch the game on TV either, even though I'd recorded it with the original plan being to relive the whole Wembley experience when we got home. I knew that dozens had also recorded it; no one had watched it yet. The pain was still too raw.

At least the *Bromley Boys* premiere at the same venue, just four days after the final, was more enjoyable. There was a parade of vintage cars around the stadium before the reception and there was the unreal experience of finding myself standing alongside Liz on the red carpet (which was actually green) posing for press photographers who probably had no idea who we were.

Not for the first time, I was squinting as I was being photographed. This time, it wasn't an attempt to look like Clint Eastwood, but the effect of flashbulbs going off yards from my face. Not something many other unemployed sixty-three-year-olds get to experience.

Afterwards, we moved inside the stadium to the Great Hall, where the screening was taking place, and took our seats near the front. I managed to sit as far from Warren, the scriptwriter, as possible. Not because I didn't like him, I did; but because we were dressed almost identically, from the dark suit down to the tan-brown brogues.

It was only when the opening scene came up that it finally hit me. This boy onscreen was me, or at least someone pretending to be me. There was one scene, where he was sitting round a table with Mum and Dad, spreading Marmite on Weetabix, complaining about how unfair everything was, which really hit home and the last fifty years just melted away. I was probably the only person in the room to find this moving (one celebrity who was sitting near me certainly didn't. She was too busy texting someone on her phone).

It was bizarre to see *EastEnders* legend Martine McCutcheon on the screen playing my mum (with Alan Davies, instead of Hugh Grant, portraying my dad). Even more bizarrely, Brenock O'Connor perfectly captured the awkwardness of the teenage me. I only wished my dad could have been there to see it – I know he would have enjoyed it. My son, Bill, and Liz certainly did.

Even when it was over and the crowd got to their feet for a standing ovation (sadly aimed at Warren, not me), I still found it hard to believe that my story had made it to film. A thought briefly crossed my mind that Bromley's triumphant return to Wembley after fifty years in the football wilderness – with its tragic denouement that no scriptwriter (not even Warren) could possibly have made up – might one day be seen in cinemas too.

It had been an exciting evening, but the long day, combined with the disappointment of Saturday and the effects of age, had taken their toll, and we went back to the hotel. Roy, Neil Smith, Jack Holland and Jeff, the club's general manager, who were made of sterner stuff, celebrated in the West End until the early hours. And all four of these would be at the Ravens Bar and Grill an hour after today's Gateshead game.

As another example of the closeness between the club and the fans, there was an annual quiz night, in which all the players took part. I was part of a team, George's Army, made up of George Porter, four of the Weavers, Half-Time John (who was married to one of the Weavers) and Frankie Raymond.

As I had a bit of time to spare before the quiz started, I went along to the club shop, where Jim was clearing away after another busy day. Mickey Crouch had tipped me off that some old memorabilia had turned up there, and I was keen to have a look.

But before that, we talked about that game at Wembley four months earlier. We were both still finding it hard to believe that Bromley had made it all the way to the FA Trophy final, after spending so many years watching some of the worst teams in the club's history.

The fact that some fans were still disappointed was testament to how far the club had come in the last fifty years. When I'd started coming to Hayes Lane, we were near the bottom of the Isthmian League. Now we were near the top of the National League. We talked about our heroes from the past; it turned out that Jim was so keen to get a couple of players to come and play for Bromley that he had paid the transfer fees himself.

Eventually, I remembered why I was there and asked him about the memorabilia that Mickey had told me about. Jim was slightly confused at first, until he realised what Mickey was talking about and pointed to a bunch of old plastic bags piled up in the corner, which looked as though they were ready to be thrown out.

I walked over and opened one of the bags, which was ripped in several places. Inside, it was carelessly crammed with old pictures, the frames covered in dust and cobwebs, with the glass on every one of them broken. But my heart rate increased as I began to recognise them, even though I hadn't seen them since the early 1970s.

These were the pictures from the wall of the tea hut, which I'd stared at while patiently queuing up for my half-time cup of tea and slice of Battenberg cake.

And there, beneath a layer of dust and with the glass cracked from corner to corner, was the picture that made my knees weaken. Even though I hadn't seen it since before my voice broke, I could remember every detail.

I wiped some of the dust off with my sleeve and saw that the photo itself was undamaged. I could clearly see Eric Fright chaired by his teammates, as George Brown stared proudly at his medal. Goalkeeper Tom Cornthwaite, a lathe worker by trade, was gazing at the Trophy in Fright's hands, while a huge bank of supporters made a dramatic backdrop to the scene.

I somehow managed to keep my emotions under control and adopted a casual tone.

'Is this for sale, Jim?' I asked.

Jim looked a bit surprised that anyone would want this ancient and broken piece of junk, but quickly recovered his poise. He was a club man at heart, and would never waste an opportunity to make a bit of money for Bromley FC.

'How does £35 sound?'

Thirty-five quid for something that had played such a huge part in my life? Something that had started me off on the long,

long road to Wembley all those years ago. Something I'd be able to clean up and get framed as a permanent reminder of my boyhood dreams, dreams that had finally come true. It didn't require much thought.

'Done,' I said.

Acknowledgements

Much gratitude is due to each of the 139 generous souls whose pledges made this book happen.

I'd also like to thank Giles Elliott, for editing the fourth book of mine in a row, and Dave Tavener, Dave Sandford, Derek Dobson, Roy Oliver, Colin Head, Dan Lambert, Richard Wager, John Self, Pete Williams, Peter Knott and Lloyd Chambers for filling in the gaps in my knowledge and memory.

Thanks, too, to David Birrell, Warren Dudley and Steve Garthwaite for reading through the material and offering their thoughts and ideas.

Finally, thanks to Neil Smith for getting Bromley to Wembley after all these years. It's been a long, long road.

Also by Dave Roberts

e-luv: an internet romance

The Bromley Boys

32 Programmes

Sad Men

Home and Away